Dear Reader:

The book you are about to [read is another St.] Martin's True Crime Libra[ry title, edited by] "the leader in true crime!" [Each title offers you a fascinating] account of the latest, most sensational crime that has captured national attention. St. Martin's is the publisher of bestselling true crime author and crime journalist Kieran Crowley, who explores the dark, deadly links between a prominent Manhattan surgeon and the disappearance of his wife fifteen years earlier in THE SURGEON'S WIFE. Suzy Spencer's BREAKING POINT guides readers through the tortuous twists and turns in the case of Andrea Yates, the Houston mother who drowned her five young children in the family's bathtub. In Edgar Award-nominated DARK DREAMS, legendary FBI profiler Roy Hazelwood and bestselling crime author Stephen G. Michaud shine light on the inner workings of America's most violent and depraved murderers. In the book you now hold, GONE FOREVER, author Diane Fanning details the shocking story behind the disappearance of Susan McFarland and the discovery of her charred remains.

St. Martin's True Crime Library gives you the stories behind the headlines. Our authors take you right to the scene of the crime and into the minds of the most notorious murderers to show you what really makes them tick. St. Martin's True Crime Library paperbacks are better than the most terrifying thriller, because it's all true! The next time you want a crackling good read, make sure it's got the St. Martin's True Crime Library logo on the spine—you'll be up all night!

Charles E. Spicer, Jr.
Executive Editor, St. Martin's True Crime Library

St. Martin's True Crime Library Titles
by Diane Fanning

BABY BE MINE

GONE FOREVER

THROUGH THE WINDOW

INTO THE WATER

WRITTEN IN BLOOD

UNDER THE KNIFE

OUT THERE

GONE FOREVER

A True Story of Marriage, Betrayal, and Murder

DIANE FANNING

St. Martin's Paperbacks

GONE FOREVER

Copyright © 2006 by Diane Fanning.

Cover photo of "Missing" poster @ William Luther/San Antonio *Express-News*.
Cover photo of Richard McFarland © Bob Owen/San Antonio *Express-News*.

ISBN: 0-312-99404-4
EAN: 9780312-99404-4

Printed in the United States of America

St. Martin's Paperbacks edition / February 2006

St. Martin's Paperbacks are published by St. Martin's Press, 175 Fifth Avenue, New York, NY 10010.

10 9 8 7 6 5 4 3

To Susan McFarland
And to the three boys she left behind

Acknowledgments

The only way a book like this one is possible is through the kindness of strangers. And now that it is finished they are strangers no more. I owe them all a debt of gratitude.

In the Bexar County District Attorney's Office, I send my appreciation to Judge Susan Reed, Michael Bernard, Catherine Babbitt, Bettina Richardson and Julian Martinez. I had looked forward to your courtroom performance—maybe next time. And thanks to the many people in that department who smiled as they saw me in the halls and made me feel welcome and at home.

In the Bexar County court systems, thanks to Gary Gauntt in the records department and Rachel Rushton, Alice Gonzales, Beatrice Gonzales and Gloria Tamayo in the district clerk's office.

A special thanks to Sergeant Shawn Palmer who proved, once again, that the Texas Rangers are an exceptional group of law enforcement professionals and you are one of the best in that elite group.

And to Detective Sergeant Boyd Wedding—may your rodeo weeks never again be interrupted by the call of duty.

In the Bexar County Medical Examiner's Office, I send my thanks to Dr. Randall Frost, in the fire marshall's office to Ted Manganello and in the Bexar County correctional center, Aida Camero with the MATCH/PATCH programs.

We all owe a debt of gratitude to Executive Director Kate Kohl and to Mary Dry of the Heidi Search Center for the special service and comfort they provide to families in our community. I also must thank Kate for her extraordinary patience and openness in explaining the work they did in the Susan McFarland case and the mission of their organization.

Thanks to Havilah Tower at the Texas Council on Family Violence for providing background information. And to the organization itself for their operation of the National Domestic Violence Hotline—800-799-SAFE.

Many thanks to neighbors, friends and acquaintances of the McFarland family including Debbie Anderson, Margot Cromack, Dee Ann Dowlen, Karen Hardeman, Carrie and Steve Miller, Molly Matthews, Mimi Riley, Linda Schlather, and Charlene and Susan Schooling. Thank you for sharing your time and your memories with me.

At Southwestern Bell Corporation, thanks to Gary Long, Phil Rodick and Kevin Jefferies for your input and the tour of Susan's workplace. I appreciate the time you took out of a very busy week.

And those of you who spoke to me but chose to remain nameless—thank you.

Of course, no acknowledgment section would be complete without thanks to my agent, Jane Dystel; Executive Editor Charles Spicer and editors Emily Drum and Joe Cleemann at St. Martin's Press; and my ever-patient, always-supportive life partner, Wayne. The five of you made this book possible.

But most of all, I want to thank Susan's brother, Pete Smith, Susan's sister, Ann Smith Carr, and Susan's niece Kirsten Slaughter. Your memories, thoughts and reflections brought Sue to life.

1

Texas Ranger Shawn Palmer and Terrell Hills Police Department Investigator Boyd Wedding drove into the hardscrabble countryside of southeast Bexar County to follow up a lead on the afternoon of January 14, 2003. Only miles from the thriving downtown of San Antonio, the eighth largest city in the United States, this rural area looked worlds away from the glitter of the Majestic Theatre and the majesty of the Cadena-Reeves Justice Center.

Palmer and Wedding traveled past well-maintained ranch homes, old farmhouses with peeling paint, seedy trailers with broken windows, overgrown fields and occasional piles of illegally dumped mattresses, broken appliances and other no longer desirable accoutrements of civilization. The investigators' destination was an abandoned farm owned by Clark Barkmeyer at 9394 South W.W. White Road. Although, as always, the two men hoped this lead would be productive, they knew they followed many to nowhere—they knew the many miles they walked to find nothing at all. They squashed their optimism under the weight of the hard lessons they had learned.

They pulled into the dusty side street. A mound of dirt blocked the end of the drive leading into the property. The owner created that barrier a short time ago to discourage trespassers. The tall dried weeds and weary buildings on the unkempt property spoke of dying dreams and shattered hope. There was no warmth and no welcome here.

Both officers headed straight for the empty house. Inside, it looked as if the last occupant woke up one morning and walked away. Clothing, small personal items and an occasional weary piece of furniture filled each room. Dust covered every surface and sparkled in the sunlight trickling through the windows. The refrigerator was well stocked, but, without electricity, its contents were rotten and rancid.

They moved trash aside searching for any place a body could be concealed. They peered into corners looking for any signs of an altercation that could point to a crime occurring inside this dwelling. Nothing raised the slightest suspicion.

Outside of the house, the two men split up down an invisible line that ran the length of the property from the road. Wedding took the right half, Palmer the left. In addition to looking for a body, they were looking for any signs of a fire—witnesses reported something burning on this land.

Flattened brown grass crunched under Palmer's feet as he walked the short distance to the detached garage just north of the residence. The double doors hung open. From the disrupted dirt scraped and mounded around the doorway, it looked as if someone had opened the door wider a short time ago.

Next, Palmer moved to the small outbuilding, thirty-six steps from the garage. It was a strange structure, slapped together with big sheets of Styrofoam insulation.

Palmer stood still and listened to the whispered sounds of movement inside. He exercised caution as he eased open the door. He was greeted by a litter of nine- to ten-week-old black puppies with white chests and tan feet squirming out of their makeshift bed to beg for attention. Scattered through this building were more signs of an impulsive departure in the past—articles of clothing, household items and other detritus of daily life.

Near this building a Datsun pickup truck bed converted into a pull-along trailer caught Palmer's eye. As he neared it, a foul odor blending the corruption of decomposition and the nauseous stench of burnt flesh drew his attention as it offended his senses. He yelled for his partner.

Wedding, meanwhile, walked a zig-zag path through the field. He found a 1988 Chevrolet Camaro stolen two days before Christmas—not in any way connected to the case they were investigating.

Then, he turned his attention to the barn. It was a derelict wooden building, appearing as if it would collapse to the ground in a light gust of wind. Hanging from the huge rafters were scythes, rakes and other farming implements ready to fall on an unsuspecting head and harvest a life.

Wedding was so focused on the barn and its contents, he did not hear the repeated calls from Palmer. He contemplated the risk of going inside. Just before he stepped across the threshold, he turned his head in his partner's direction. Palmer saw the movement and windmilled his arms in the air.

As Wedding headed toward him, Palmer took a closer look at the trailer. On the surface of the rubble in the bed were wires and the metal skeletons of electronic devices marred by flames and rust—perhaps the television and VCR reportedly gone from the missing woman's Explorer.

Beneath that debris, Palmer spotted what he both hoped and dreaded he would find—the curve of human rib bones, an upper arm bone and the roundness of a shoulder. The surfaces were crusty, cracked and browned, but still the bones screamed out their humanity. He confirmed this deduction when his eyes found the unmistakable shape of a human skull.

He looked closer at the pyre and saw metal springs. Then his eye caught an interesting piece of litter tucked in the corner. It was plastic packaging, curled and puckered from the heat—a strip of wrappers that once held Wyler's Authentic Italian Ices. Palmer knew their suspect, Richard McFarland, was obsessed with this snack. And he knew he found the missing woman.

He walked toward the approaching Wedding. "I found her," he said.

"Where's she at?" Wedding asked.

Pointing, Palmer answered, "Over there in the trailer."

Wedding approached, taking great care not to touch or

disturb any possible evidence. He looked hard at the contents, but could not identify anything that looked human. Palmer pointed out the curves of the charred bones and then Wedding, too, knew the fate of Sue McFarland. The hunt was over.

2

Former judge and Bexar County District Attorney Susan D. Reed sat in a burgundy leather executive's chair embossed with the seal of Texas in her office on the fifth floor of the Cadena-Reeves Justice Center in downtown San Antonio. Perched above the city streets, through the windows to her left, she was at steeple level with the historic San Fernando Cathedral. The cornerstone for this city landmark was laid in 1738. Construction was completed in 1755, making it the first parish church in Texas. Those original walls still stood and formed the sanctuary of the current edifice.

Across the street from the Cathedral, a swatch of green and a shooting fountain broke the concrete monotony of the city streets. Tall brick and sandstone buildings created a red backdrop on the skyline.

From the window behind her, she looked across the street at the massive Romanesque Revival architecture of native Texas granite and red sandstone—the old Bexar County Courthouse, built in the 1890s. The new justice center that housed her office was connected to the older building by a tunnel that ran under Main Street.

Inside, a wooden desk with a light layer of clutter sat in front of Reed. The wall she faced was covered with photographs taken of her with other important Texas personalities like both Presidents Bush and Barbara Bush, Senator Kay Bailey Hutchison and Governor Rick Perry. Scattered throughout the display of photos were framed magazine covers featuring the district attorney's determined face.

To her left, a bookcase stretched along the wall. As expected, its shelves held a complete set of *Vernon's Annotated Texas Codes* as well as other legal guides. The personal side of the D.A. lightened the weight of the serious tomes— photographs of her son from babyhood to adulthood; CDs by Norah Jones, Carly Simon and Lou Rawls; a few eclectic books like *Capone* by John Kobler, *Grudge Match* by San Antonio author Jay Brandon and Frommer's *Born to Shop Paris.*

A herd of elephants trumpeting her political allegiance stampeded through her office in every size, shape and design imaginable, including a colorful Oaxacan wood carving from Mexico. The whimsical touches continued with items like a Texas Prison Rodeo cap, a bottle of Victory over Evil oil and a basketful of cascarones, the colorful confetti-filled eggs that were ever-present during the Fiesta celebration in April each year.

Reed's cell phone, as usual, was tucked down in her purse. Most days, though, she had it set to vibrate and never noticed when someone called. Not today.

When the phone rang just after 2 P.M., she fumbled in her handbag until her fingers locked around the keypad. She extracted it from a bundle of miscellany and pressed the TALK button.

"I'm out here in a field and I think I've found her," Texas Ranger Shawn Palmer said.

He didn't need to say more. Reed knew who he meant. It was mid-January and everyone had been looking for Susan McFarland since Thanksgiving. Everyone except Richard McFarland.

Reed wanted to rush to the scene to see it all first-hand, but she had her job to do. First, the three young sons of Susan McFarland needed to be spirited away from the family nome to a secure location. Next, Richard McFarland needed to be cuffed, arrested and questioned once again. She had no doubt about his guilt. Now, she just needed to prove it.

3

Steven Hanson, the chief medical investigator for the Bexar County Medical Examiner's Office, arrived at the scene at 3:05 P.M. He observed the contents of the trailer. He agreed with investigators that the Texas Department of Public Safety's Crime Laboratory Service personnel should process the scene before the damaged body was transported in for an autopsy. He left two body bags and two clean white sheets and instructed officers on the proper procedure for collecting the remains and the surrounding debris.

While the Texas Department of Protective and Regulatory Services was ensuring the safety of the three McFarland boys, Sergeant Palmer was drawing up paperwork. He would not serve any warrant until he knew the boys were removed, to prevent them from becoming possible hostages if McFarland decided to flee. He prepared the three affidavits he hoped would result in arrest warrants for Richard McFarland. He presented his case to Judge Sid Harle of the 226th District Court. The judge issued three warrants on charges of unauthorized use of a vehicle, tampering with a witness and tampering with or fabricating physical evidence. Murder charges could not be filed until the medical examiner confirmed the identity of the charred body and made a ruling on the cause and manner of death.

While waiting for word on the safety of the children, Sergeant Palmer and Investigator Wedding kept McFarland under surveillance. They were parked in a lot at Interstate 35 and Dolorosa Street when they received information that McFarland was heading out to pick up his oldest son and go to his lawyer's office.

In the heavy downtown traffic congestion, the two officers wound up a block ahead of their quarry by the time they got the go-ahead for the arrest. They slowed down and allowed McFarland to move ahead of them on St. Mary's Street near Commerce Street. Palmer pulled up beside McFarland's white Windstar van. Then he whipped his vehicle in front of McFarland and slammed on his brakes. The suspect honked his horn in annoyance.

Palmer and Wedding approached opposite sides of the van with guns drawn. Since they were not wearing uniforms, the two armed men looked more like carjackers than law enforcement to many of the drivers and pedestrians on the scene.

In locked elbow stance, they ordered McFarland to get out of the van. McFarland unlocked the driver's-side door, but did not move. Palmer opened the door and repeated his request. Still, McFarland did not move. Palmer eased him out of the car, cuffed his hands behind him and put him in the back seat of his official vehicle. Palmer drove McFarland over to the Justice Center, and Wedding followed behind the wheel of McFarland's van. McFarland appeared apathetic and disinterested. He asked no questions. He offered no answers. Inside the Windstar, Wedding was jubilant.

In the courtroom, Judge Harle set bond at $150,000 for each charge—a total of $450,000. Before the bench, McFarland mumbled about an attorney—speaking out when he should have been silent and remaining mute when it was appropriate to speak. Palmer delivered McFarland to the nearby Bexar County correction center, where sheriff's department personnel confirmed the warrants. Then they booked and processed their prisoner and escorted McFarland to his cell.

Living in a home with three young boys was a noisy proposition that prepared McFarland for almost any decibel level of sound—but it did not prepare him for the constant din of jail. Behind bars, the voices never stopped shouting in his ears. The thumps and bangs of masses of men crowded into confined spaces beat like a drum in his head. The slamming of metal doors reverberated in his ears long after the entry was shut.

4

Oxford, Mississippi, was home base for Mary Elizabeth Mitchell's family. In fact, her great-grandfather, T. D. Isom, founded the town and was a leader in the establishment of the University of Mississippi—"Ole Miss"—there. Mary Elizabeth's parents moved to St. Louis for a while, where she was born. Then they moved back to their home state.

Mary Elizabeth was not a typical young woman of the 1930s. After high school, she continued her education at Belhaven College in Jackson, Mississippi, and went on to earn a bachelor's degree from the University of Mississippi in Oxford in 1940. From there, she pursued a master's degree in social work from Tulane University in New Orleans.

Huck Smith's family hailed from Indianola, Mississippi, southwest of Oxford. His dad was 68 years old when Huck was born. He was just 8 years old when his father died and his mother moved the family back to her hometown of New Orleans.

After getting his undergraduate degree in accounting from Loyola, Huck went to law school at Tulane during the day. By night, he worked as a transcriber for the FBI. It was here in the Big Easy that Miss Minnie—Huck's cousin and Mary Elizabeth's friend—introduced the couple. They were married in June of 1942.

Huck left law school to work full-time for the FBI and Mary Elizabeth never got around to writing her dissertation. Huck's job transfers moved them to Seattle, Los Angeles and finally, St. Louis. The couple endeared themselves to family and friends. Huck loved to entertain others with his jokes and storytelling. Mary Elizabeth, with her natural proclivity for organization, shared her skills and tips with anyone who was interested. Visitors to their home always felt welcome. Huck and Mary Elizabeth dropped everything to make sure their guests had a good time.

By the time they moved to the St. Louis area in 1956, they had three children: Harley, Ann and Pete. Their fourth and final child was born on New Year's Eve in 1958 when Mary Elizabeth was 40, Huck 48 and the other three children were 15, 13 and 11.

Mary Elizabeth loved the name Susan, so the first name of the new baby girl was not up for debate. The siblings lobbied for a middle name that started with an "O." They wanted their little sister's initials to spell out "S.O.S." In the end, they lost that battle—the new addition to the family was Susan Burris Smith.

As she grew up, her brothers and sister would often tease her that she was an accident. She always quipped back, "No, I'm a bonus!" Huck, an FBI agent, received a letter of congratulations from FBI Director J. Edgar Hoover upon the birth of his daughter. That letter would later be framed along with a picture of Huck and hung with pride in Susan's own home.

Sue grew up on Newport Avenue in Webster Groves, Missouri. Older sister Ann got saddled with all the baby-sitting duty for her kid sister. In that era, watching over little ones was girls' work and not something a red-blooded, all-American boy would even be asked to do. At times, Ann resented that her brothers did not have to share in the responsibility.

By the time Sue was three, Ann discovered that it was fun to spend time with her little sister. She was cute, easy-tempered and affectionate. Ann even took her along on dates on occasion. One time, Ann and a date had Sue along with them at Blackburn Park. Sue got a little bit annoying. Ann's date picked her up, swung her around and dumped her in a trash can. Sue giggled with delight and the two teenagers laughed along with her.

As soon as Ann and Sue got in the front door, Sue made a beeline for her mother. "Mom, they put me in a trash can over there."

Ratted out by her little sister. Ann thought she would never hear the end of that from her mother.

When Ann went off to college, she often had Sue up to spend the weekend. The other girls at the all-women's school doted on Sue. It was like having a little pet around.

At the same time, Sue was enchanting her older sister's friends, she was also developing a relationship with a younger relative. Sue's brother Harley had a daughter, Kirsten, who was born five years after Sue. When Kirsten was 3, she was left with her grandmother—Sue's mom, Mary Elizabeth—for a month and a half while her parents were overseas.

Mary Elizabeth told Sue she would give her a quarter if she would keep Kirsten entertained. Sue took her niece's hand in hers and went off to play. A few minutes later she stomped back with her charge in tow. "Mom, I don't want a quarter."

It wasn't a great relationship then, but as time passed the two girls grew as close as sisters. One of Kirsten's favorite memories was the time she went to summer camp when she was 10 years old. Sue sent her a huge five-pound box of candy. After that shipment arrived, Kirsten was the most popular girl in the cabin.

Sue was 12 years old when her brother Pete married Debbie. Her new sister-in-law remembered an active, vivacious little girl who loved to play board games. Eight years later, when a divorced Debbie was visiting her parents in St. Louis, Sue threw the same enthusiasm into trying to set Debbie up with a date.

At the age of 13, a mutual friend introduced Sue to Sandy Rowe. The two girls went to different schools—Sue at Steger Junior High and Sandy at Hixson Junior High—but they became fast friends just the same. They were a regular sight at the bakery in Warson Woods, where they both got hooked on the oversized sugar cookies with bright yellow icing decorated with smiley faces. In tenth grade, they both attended Webster Groves High School and the girls became constant companions.

Sue worked as a lifeguard at hotel swimming pools in the summer. When the pools were not busy, Sandy would keep her company playing endless games of two-handed spades.

Sandy was drawn to Sue by her infectious *joie de vivre*—just being around her chased both blues and ennui away. Sue was active and energetic, always ready to go, go, go. Sitting around watching TV did not suit her. She wanted to fill every minute with fun. If Sandy was content to just hang out and do nothing, Sue wheedled, "C'mon, Sandy. C'mon," till Sandy relented and never regretted doing so.

Sue and Sandy watched an endless stream of movies and shopped for hours on end. Sue loved tennis and tried in vain to teach Sandy, but her friend just couldn't get the hang of it.

In addition to tennis and swimming, Sue loved ice skating at the community rink and was a hockey cheerleader in her sophomore and junior years. She liked less physical pursuits as well—serving on the Student Council and in the Pep and French Clubs.

She also was an avid reader. Sandy, like most of the students in Honors English was a reader, too. But she was in awe of Sue, who would race through one large paperback after another as if she were determined to read every book ever published.

At first blush, Sue Smith sounded like the perfect teenager. But she was no paragon of virtue. Her rebellious side drove her into verbal sparring matches with her mother with great frequency. She even cut class or went home for lunch and intentionally returned late to school.

As an adolescent, Sue could lie like a professional con artist. She made up elaborate and credible stories to explain her absences and tardiness. When adults fell for her tall tales, she and Sandy would laugh about them for days.

Of all Sue's excuses, one of Sandy's favorites was the fish disaster.

Sue rushed breathless into the classroom one morning. "I'm so sorry I'm late," she told the teacher. "The fish tank in my house broke and the fish were flopping all over the floor." Of course, she continued, she'd simply had to rescue the creatures and clean up the mess before she returned to school.

The teenager was also a master at creative manipulation. During her junior year, she had a desperate desire to get a second piercing in her ear. In the mid-seventies, double-piercing was still considered a bit edgy, and Sue's mom said no.

Time for plan B. Sue convinced Sandy to get *her* ears double-pierced—going so far as to offer to pay for the procedure and call it a birthday present. "Then, I'll take you home and show my mom and she'll think it's okay because she likes you," Sue said.

Sandy agreed and the plan worked. After Sandy demonstrated her double-piercing to Sue's mother, Mary Smith relented and gave her blessing for Sue to do the same.

Sue and Sandy graduated from Webster Groves High School in 1977. Sue continued her education at William Woods University, a private girls' college in Fulton, Missouri. Sandy stayed in St. Louis and lived on campus at Washington University while working at Southwestern Bell to take advantage of the tuition plan to pay for her schooling. The two friends were separated, but only by an hour-and-a-half drive, and they visited each other a lot.

Sandy was shocked at first when Sue announced she was majoring in Accounting. Like many people, Sandy's stereotype of an accountant was a stick-in-the-mud nerd with no sense of humor—not anywhere near the personality of her friend. The more she thought about it, though, the more it made sense. Sue was a cut-up, but she was also disciplined, organized and concrete—all qualities that would serve her well in her chosen career.

Her career choice surprised her brother Pete, too. He'd always imagined Sue becoming a teacher because she had so much energy. Then he remembered that his dad had a degree in accounting and Sue—like all of her siblings—deeply admired Huck Smith.

Sue's family gathered in Fulton to watch Sue walk across the stage and accept her diploma from William Woods in 1981. The announcer at last reached her name. "Susan Burris Smith, *cum laude*."

For a second, her family sat in stunned silence. *Cum laude*? Sue never mentioned that. Then they burst into a roar of approval. Most of the family had not appreciated how bright Sue was. Her playful—never serious—demeanor hid a quick and agile mind.

Immediately upon graduation, Sue accepted an accounting position with Sante Fe Energy in Amarillo, Texas, and it was there that she acquired her CPA. She found another important life-friendship out in the panhandle of Texas with Dee Ann, another single woman and co-worker at the oil company. Sue rented a little house with a couple of friends just up the street from where Dee Ann lived with her young son. Sue often went up the street for a dip in Dee Ann's swimming pool and soon they were fast friends, spending many a night at Steak 'n' Ale together.

Sue made a special trip from Amarillo to St. Louis that year to serve as maid of honor as her best friend stood at the altar and became Sandy Horn. Sandy never visited Sue in far-flung Amarillo, but they kept in touch by telephone and saw each other when Sue came to St. Louis to visit her parents.

It was a time when Sandy needed the support of Sue, and her friend did not let her down. In the four and a half years her marriage lasted, Sandy turned to Sue for a good ear and even better advice.

Sue's next job took her to the dusty west Texas town of Midland. Her employer was Enron. At the time the company had an impeccable reputation, but at the turn of the millennium, scandal exposed a network of lies and misrepresentations, and led to its downfall. After six months, Enron transferred her to the company's headquarters in the sprawling metropolis of Houston.

There Sue renewed her friendship with her former sister-in-law Debbie. Sue went to her nephews' soccer games and accompanied Debbie and her kids on trips to Galveston island.

Of course, she and Debbie went shopping together. Sue made the experience a non-stop adventure in fun. In stores, she exhibited the awe of a child, amazed at all the new items that caught her eye.

She built up quite a closetful of evening outfits. She augmented her bounty through a cooperative mailing exchange with her girlfriends in Amarillo. They shipped clothing back and forth, expanding their wardrobes exponentially.

In late 1987, Sue accepted a position in St. Louis with Southwestern Bell Corporation in the Yellow Pages division. Right before her move back home, she took a trip out to Amarillo to serve as maid of honor in Dee Ann's wedding to George Dowlen on November 26, 1987.

Dee Ann was marrying a man with quite a reputation. After George spent a ten-year stint as a prosecutor in neighboring Randall County, Governor Dolph Brisco appointed him to the 181st District Court in Amarillo. From that seat, Dowlen quickly earned the moniker of "the cowboy judge with the Boston brain." He was best known in Texas for presiding over one of the murder trials of multimillionaire oilman T. Cullen Davis. Media flooded the courtroom, in part because of the wealth of the defendant, but also because of the notoriety of the defense counsel—flamboyant Houston lawyer Racehorse Haynes. By the time the verdict was read, this trial was the longest and one of the most controversial in the state's history.

Now this judge was making personal history of his own with his first trip to the altar. For his bride, it was round two. The couple invited Sue to stay with them for the remainder of the weekend. No one anticipated the heavy snow that whipped through the Texas Panhandle on the Dowlens' wedding night. Sue was snowbound with the newlyweds for days.

Back in St. Louis, Sue flew into a social whirl of dinner

parties, gallery openings and charitable society events, including The Veiled Prophet Ball, an annual autumn fund-raising gala since 1878. The earliest incarnation of the fictional Veiled Prophet resembled a member of the Ku Klux Klan. He wore a white sheet and a pointed hat with a pistol in one hand and a shotgun in the other.

For years, the organization catered to the elite, the powerful and the wealthy—exclusively white and committed to the maintenance of the status quo. Each year, one of the community's leading citizens donned the title and the garb, his identity sworn to secrecy.

When change came, it was not gradual. It was forced into being in 1972. Tom K. Smith, an executive at Monsanto was the prophet that year. He took the seat of honor with his veil firmly in place.

Gena Scott, a white civil rights activist with ACTION (Action Committee to Improve Opportunities for Negroes) ascended unseen up to the balcony. There she grabbed a power cable, swung out from her perch and slid down its length. When she reached the Veiled Prophet, she unveiled him with one smooth twist of the wrist. Smith, his bald head and secret identity exposed, seethed with anger.

It was a wake-up call for St. Louis and the charitable organization. Integration of the ranks began. By the time Sue arrived back in her hometown, the group was as diverse as the city itself.

By 1995, its chairman was Horace Wilkins, an African-American executive at Southwestern Bell Corporation. In 2003, the Grand Marshall of the parade was Ossie Smith, a celebrated African-American actor and civil rights activist.

Living in the same city once again, Sue and Sandy drifted back into old patterns of behavior and shared confidences. Only now, after they finished with mutual tea and sympathy, Sue did not drag Sandy out for tennis or a movie or a couple of smiley-faced cookies—instead she pulled her along to aerobics class.

Now that Sue and her niece Kirsten were both older, the

age difference became irrelevant. The two often went out together in the evening or on weekends. Sue, being more established in her career than the younger Kirsten, had more disposable income. Because of that, Sue's ideas for fun often exceeded Kirsten's budget. Sue told her to come along anyway and never hesitated to pay her niece's way.

But time was ticking away loud and clear in Sue's mind as her 30th birthday loomed large at year's end. She was worried that she would never find the right guy, and her dream of children would go unfulfilled. She told Dee Ann that she wanted to be a stay-at-home mom with a whole bunch of kids and a loving husband who worked to support them all.

In late 1988, Sue went to a party and met a young successful stockbroker named Richard Marvin McFarland.

5

Dick and Mona McFarland, natives of Kirkwood, Missouri, married and started their family in time to be part of the post-war Baby Boom. Dick worked at Monsanto and Mona stayed home with her boys.

Their second son, Richard Marvin McFarland was born on May 23, 1957, in Pennsylvania. Soon after, the family moved back to the St. Louis area and Rick was raised in Webster Groves on Lee Avenue with two brothers, David and Don.

As typical in many families at that time, Dick was not a day-to-day hands-on father. He did, however, carve out some time for his boys. Rick cherished these memories all his life.

He recalled his dad lying on the floor, placing his feet in Rick's small tummy and hoisting him in the air, declaring, "Kitty in the tree. Kitty in the tree." He remembered Indian Guides—a program sponsored by the YMCA to foster positive bonds between fathers and sons—and the days when his dad was Big Silver Feather and he was Little Silver Feather. They made a wooden eagle totem pole lamp together.

Another special memory began at the S Bar F Scout Ranch, where Rick killed a timberback rattlesnake with a rock. Dick helped his son mount the snake skin on a large wood plank, chiseling out an indentation for the snake's rattles and covering it in Plexiglas.

Rick recalled the two of them whittling and sanding a Pinewood Derby race car as a Cub Scout project for Pack

301. The expert craftsman and the small unskilled boy worked in tandem to win first place in the Best Looking and in the Most Unique Design categories. A number of years later, Dick and Rick worked on their "cream puff" project, refurbishing a classic '55 Chevy.

Despite these times together, those who knew the family thought Dick was an emotionally remote father—he was hard on Rick, pushing his son beyond his capabilities. Rick pushed himself, too—always desperate to please his dad.

But the major influence over the lives of these three boys was wielded by their mother, Mona. She ruled the home front with a judgmental, self-righteous and rigid form of Christian fundamentalism.

Rick attended Webster Groves High School, where he played water polo, worked on sound and light crews for theater productions and was a member of the staff of the school newspaper, the *Echo*. He graduated in 1975. Sue's good friend Sandy, Class of '77, remembered him as "a pretty happening, popular, hang-with-the-cheerleaders kind of guy."

Rick continued his education at Southwest Missouri State University in Springfield. He was challenged by difficulty with paying attention and maintaining concentration. He had to work hard to earn a "B" average. The only known blemish on his record was an accusation that he'd stolen property from a friend at school. Ultimately, that charge was dismissed.

He graduated in 1980 with a bachelor's degree in Business Administration and got a job at Shearson Lehman, a reputable stock brokerage company. Rick did well there. He drove a BMW and lived in a lovely old carriage house in a very nice part of town.

In 1984, when a group of prominent civic-minded single men formed the St. Louis Squires and Ladies, Rick was quick to join. The organization was a foundation that sought out civic, cultural and charitable projects not helped by traditional funding sources. The group planned a variety of entertainment events from black-tie balls to scavenger hunts to raise these funds. In addition to their charitable work, the organization was an excellent venue for professional and personal networking.

Warning signs of possible instability were well hidden—most of the time. But not to one woman Rick dated. She said that after a couple of dates, she was very uncomfortable with him. She informed him that she was no longer interested in pursuing a relationship.

Rick, she claimed, would not stop calling her. The many calls were troubling, but she considered them nothing more than a nuisance for a while. Then, it all became serious. She felt threatened and frightened when she caught Rick lurking in the bushes outside of her home.

In 1988, Rick met Susan Smith at a party. Although they'd lived in the same town and attended the same high school, this encounter was their first.

6

"I went to a party in St. Louis and ran into Rick McFarland from high school. Do you remember him?" Sue asked.

Sandy hadn't really known Rick, but she knew who he was, and he had even dated another friend of hers. Rick was a year older and considered a good catch as a high school boyfriend.

Nonetheless, it surprised Sue's large circle of friends when the two started dating. It stunned them how quickly it developed into a serious relationship. They wondered if he was right for her, and could not see what she saw in him.

Rick was a lot more reserved than Sue. He was a nice, steady guy. But he wasn't very quick-witted. He was always the slowest in any group to catch a joke—if he got it at all.

Sue, on the other hand, was bright, strong-willed, passionate and tempestuous. In time, Sandy saw Rick as a counterbalance to Sue—able to tether the high soaring balloon of her emotions.

Kirsten thought Sue was settling for less than she deserved. She believed her aunt wanted marriage and children enough that she was willing to overlook a lot.

Another friend said, "Sue is a superwoman—very productive, very efficient, a very take-charge person, and Rick wasn't like that at all. But we thought maybe he was the yin to her yang."

Beneath the personality differences, though, Rick and

Sue did have a lot in common. Both were raised in Webster Groves and shared a core of Midwestern values. The two were social animals as well—loving parties and time spent with friends. Rick looked like the answer to Sue's dream of being married with children.

Over the July Fourth weekend, the couple traveled to Amarillo to spend time with Sue's friend Dee Ann and her new husband, George Dowlen. The Dowlens thought Rick was nice, but his stuttering when he got excited accentuated his social awkwardness. Another of her Amarillo friends doubted that Sue was in love, but one look at the couple and it was obvious that both of them were very happy and excited about getting married.

Sue always loved having bright colors all around her. Her special wedding gift request was red enamel pots and pans for her kitchen.

After years of working at Shearson Lehman, Rick switched to another stock brokerage firm, Stifel Nicolaus in July 1989. The future looked bright.

Days before the wedding, a distressed Sue called her sister Ann to tell her Rick had changed jobs.

"Why does that upset you?" Ann asked.

"He changed jobs three weeks ago and I just found out."

Rick's mother, Mona, was disappointed about the impending marriage. Sue was not who they thought Rick would—or should—marry. Mona saw Sue as a good-time party girl and did not approve of her at all. Sue's mother, Mary Elizabeth, had her reservations about the match, too. Mona and Mary Elizabeth met, but could not relate to one another. Their backgrounds, outlooks on life and lifestyle were as disparate as if one of them had come from the fjords of Norway and the other from sub-Saharan Africa.

Despite the misgivings of family and friends, the couple married at Webster Groves Presbyterian Church on August 12, 1989. It was a weekend-long event with a rehearsal dinner and a bridal lunch. The large and elaborate ceremony had eight tuxedoed groomsmen, eight bridesmaids—including friends Dee Ann and Sandy—and four hundred guests.

The ever practical Sue chose bridesmaid dresses that could be worn again. She selected a tailored two-piece pattern with puffy short sleeves, a daring neckline and a straight mid-calf skirt slit to the knee. Then she purchased a textured black fabric and hired a seamstress to sew up the provocative ensembles. Rick wore a tuxedo and Susan a simple crème silk gown. The reception was in an historic house near St. Louis. Hors d'oeuvres and cocktails were served. A small string quartet played in the stairwell. Bridesmaid Sandy said, "It was like a fairy tale."

Rick and Sue set up housekeeping in Olivette, Missouri. Rick took Sue by surprise again. She shared her shock and dismay with her sister when she discovered that her new husband brought a mountain of debt with him into the marriage. Before the ceremony, she hadn't had a clue. It took years to pay it all off.

In December, Sue was promoted to local and national billing management at Southwestern Bell's Yellow Pages division. Meantime, Rick, after six short months of less than stellar performance, left Stifel Nicolaus and accepted a real estate investment position with Paragon Realty. That job, too, did not last long. In six months, he moved on to insurance sales at Aetna, where he lasted a year.

While working those jobs, Rick bugged his sister-in-law and brother-in-law for access to their co-workers. No matter how many times the two told him it would not be appropriate for them to invite him to their workplaces to make a sales pitch, Rick continued to push. Ann was aghast the day he just dropped by because he was in the area. She hustled him out as quickly as possible.

Early in 1991, it was Sandy's turn to leave St. Louis and move to New Jersey. Sue and Rick threw an elaborate going-away party for her. Even though Sue was nine months pregnant and due any day, she went all out for the celebration—cooking and baking mountains of delectables as if obsessed with trying everything in her recipe file. Throughout the party, though, the physical stress on Sue was obvious. She was often spotted sitting down in the stairwell. When Rick walked into her vicinity, she'd ask him to rub her back.

Sue and Sandy's friendship continued to flourish despite the obstacle of physical separation. Now that Sue was back in St. Louis, the two women were able to get together whenever Sandy visited her family.

On March 1, 1991, after intense back labor, Sue gave birth to her first child at St. Luke's Hospital. Sue called him William[1] because, she said, "I've liked everyone I ever met with that name."

She hoped that a grandchild would warm up her relationship with her mother-in-law, Mona. She was disappointed. If anything the gritty association grew more abrasive. Mona disapproved of Sue working now that she was a mother. Her litany of judgmental pronouncements of Sue's abilities as a mother, a wife and a woman were never-ending.

Rick and Sue took a trip out to Amarillo to show off their new baby. Both displayed shameless delight in their new roles as parents. They were simply crazy about their son.

That summer, the family of three vacationed on Cape Cod with Kirsten, Kirsten's mom and Kirsten's boyfriend. William was a contented baby willing to go everywhere with a smile—and with a mom like Sue, they were going all the time. He was even well-behaved in restaurants. Sue plopped the baby-carrier on the table and he gurgled happily as the adults dined.

Soon after William's birth, their happiness was rocked when the couple's financial stability took a hit. Rick lost his job and was unemployed for fifteen months. As much as he wanted to succeed, he always undermined his own aspirations. With Sue's assistance he finally got a job with

---

[1] The names of Susan McFarland's children have been changed to protect their privacy.

Southwestern Bell Yellow Pages in telemarketing sales in September 1992.

Rick developed a strange habit while working there. In this position, his work station was a cubicle. But whenever his boss was out, he'd gather up the items on his desk and move them to the conference room. He'd meet with clients there as if it were his office. At times, he'd even invite friends to visit him in his "office," where he'd pretend he was in charge.

In late fall of 1992, both Rick and Sue worked for Southwestern Bell when they left their new baby with relatives to travel to Pittsburgh for Sandy's second wedding. In January 1993, they went to nearby St. Louis for Kirsten's wedding. Kirsten went to a hairdresser in the morning to have her makeup and hair done. When she came home, she was in tears. Too much makeup. Too much hair. She thought she did not look like herself at all. In fact, she thought she looked like a drag queen. Sue came to the rescue. She dried her tears. Calmed her nerves. Fixed her face and restyled her hair. Thanks to Sue, Kirsten walked down the aisle with a smile.

In Olivette, the McFarlands shared a driveway with their next-door neighbors, Margot and Doug Cromack. Rick and Sue both parked BMWs there. You couldn't miss Sue's car—its bright orange exterior drew as much attention as a streaker in the mall. Margot and Sue also shared overlapping pregnancies—both their first and second. With children the same age, Margot and Sue spent a lot of time together. Margot didn't know how Sue found the time to be active in a cooking club and a book club, on top of her job and her responsibilities as a wife and mother, but there seemed to be no end to Sue's energy. Margot thought Sue was the happiest, most optimistic person she had ever known.

Together at home, the families shared cookouts, pumpkin carvings, birthday cakes and other family traditions. Sue painted Margot's daughter's room. Margot planted Sue's rosebushes.

They lived near the St. Louis Zoo and took their children there often. In the summer, the zoo was open until 7 and was the perfect activity after work to wear the kids out before putting them to bed.

Another favorite excursion was Grant's Farm, the 281-acre ancestral home of the Busch family—of Budweiser fame—just south of St. Louis. Now it was home to more than 1,000 animals in more than 100 species from six continents—and admission was free.

Doug was in the middle of his medical residency and had little time to spend at home or with his young son. Rick filled in the gap—including the Cromack boy with William whenever Rick taught his son about guy things like how to use a screwdriver or other simple tools of household repair. When the two boys were toddlers, it was common to see the be-diapered duo pushing their bubble mowers behind Rick whenever he mowed the lawn.

In July of 1993, Rick came home from work and told Sue he was fired unfairly. He claimed the timing was deliberate—he was just two days from his one-year anniversary, when he would be eligible to file a union grievance. Sue believed him, and was furious.

She called her favorite attorney, her sister Ann. "We need a good employment attorney. Do you know one?"

Ann cautioned her, "If they fired him knowing that you are an executive with the firm, there may be more to the story. Look into this further and know what the facts are before you do anything."

Further investigation revealed that two employees had asked to be moved to another department because they did not want to work with Rick. Two others said that if management did not get rid of Rick, they would quit.

When the supervisor finally pulled the plug, Rick's reaction was so intense, he frightened her. She asked to be escorted to and from her car for an extended period of time after his dismissal.

After a couple of months of unemployment, Rick landed a job in telemarketing sales with Maritz. He then drifted over to Passport, where he sold dining cards. One day, he came home driving a brand-new Mercedes. When Sue asked, Rick told her that his boss gave it to him. Sue was disturbed—his explanation just did not sound right. Worried that he'd done something unscrupulous or criminal, she insisted he return the car. After six months with Passport, Rick moved on to Dining à la Card, followed, in a short time, by a position at Transmedia, where he continued in dining and financial services.

On September 6, 1993, their second son, James, was born in the same hospital as his brother.

Sue's next pregnancy was not successful. Between three and four months, she lost the baby—the miscarriage a result of a genetic defect. It broke Sue's heart to hear that the anomaly was more common in girls than boys. Sue wanted a girl so much—when she bought American Girl dolls for her nieces, she also bought one for herself.

Boy number three, Timothy—Timmy—arrived on March 4, 1997. He wasn't a girl, but she loved him just the same.

Ann looked at her three nephews and realized it was payback time for her little sister. Ann always sought out educational toys for kids, but Sue's philosophy was that toys were supposed to be fun. For years, Sue filled Ann's home with the noisiest, messiest toys she could find.

Now Ann got her revenge. Not only did she give the three boys loud and sloppy toys, she also took advantage of Sue's little phobia about bugs. Ann made sure her nephews had a steady supply of plastic spiders, worms and other creepy, crawly critters.

In May 1998, Sue moved up the corporate ladder again to the Budget, Forecast and Plan Preparation group at Southwestern Bell Yellow Pages. She stayed in that position for four years.

The possibility of change swirled in Sue's corporate world, jarring her sense of security with the company. An upcoming consolidation with Pac Bell threatened her position. It was possible that when the transaction was complete, she would either be unemployed or be forced to transfer to San Francisco to keep her job. She knew that city, with its high cost of living, was not ideal for a one-income family.

Sue got busy looking for openings in alternative positions in the company.

In the midst of this turmoil, Sue and Rick, without the boys, traveled to visit their former next-door neighbors, Doug and Margot Cromack, who had moved to San Antonio a year and a half earlier upon completion of Doug's residency. Sue and Rick liked the city right away.

And no wonder. It was early spring—the most perfect time of year for this part of Texas. The weather was warm, but not hot. The sun beat down with more intensity than they ever felt at the higher latitude of St. Louis, chasing the chill right out of their upcountry skin. The summertime—when temperatures hit 100 degrees, the nighttime air bore no trace of cool and the pre-dawn humidity felt like a blast from God's dryer vent—was still a couple of months away.

The Cromacks drove them all around town and out into the surrounding hill country where wildflowers bloomed in a profusion so dense it made butterflies weep with joy. One exploration of the romance of the Riverwalk sealed the deal—this was a place where Sue and Rick could envision a renewal of their spirits and their relationship.

Since Southwestern Bell had moved their corporate headquarters from St. Louis to San Antonio a couple of years earlier, Sue felt confident that she would be able to get transferred to a position there. She also was delighted at the prospect of putting a little bit of distance between herself and her mother-in-law.

Sue went to the company offices and looked at the job board. She applied for a position she found appealing and went in for an interview. Meanwhile Rick got a job offer with San Antonio's Transportation Display, selling ad space on buses.

Sue returned to Missouri to sell the house and prepare for a move. Rick moved into the room over the Cromacks' garage. Sue just missed the high times of Fiesta—an annual ten-day party that's pure San Antonio. The non-stop catalogue of events highlighted all the cultural influences that built the city—from a Mariachi Mass at the historic San Fernando Cathedral to the Fiesta Gartenfest with its beer and polka.

The major events of Fiesta never changed. The first day always included the Fiesta Oyster Bake at St. Mary's University. NIOSA, Night In Old San Antonio, filled La Villita—the original village that became San Antonio—with a four-night orgy of international food and multicultural music.

The Coronation of the Queen of the Order of the Alamo added pomp to the festivities—young women in ornate beaded gowns with heavy trains trailing in their wake. Then, the alternative entertainment of the Cornynation turned the tables on the traditional formality by making fun of it all.

The Battle of Flowers Parade wound through the streets of downtown. But the most anticipated event for many in the city was the Texas Cavaliers River Parade. The Texas Cavaliers were founded in 1926 to preserve and promote the ideals of the heroes of the Alamo and encourage good horsemanship. In modern times, they had transformed into an organization of 450 business, community and civic leaders whose foundation funded children's charities in the city. The River Parade was a significant fund-raiser for the group.

Professionally decorated barges floated down the river under a starry sky bedecked with thousands of twinkling lights and filled with people in colorful costumes.

There were 17,000 reserved tickets for sale each year, but most of the 250,000 spectators viewed the parade from restaurants, hotels, bridges and open public areas along the river. Rick saw the parade with the Cromacks from the enviable perch of a law firm overlooking the Riverwalk at a party hosted by one of the Cromacks' neighbors.

During the weeks Rick stayed at the Cromacks', they noticed odd habits that they'd not seen in the past. Rick did not seem to have a biological time clock. He often was up all night and asleep all day. Many mornings they'd rise and, noticing the glow of the overhead fluorescent lights in the room, they'd check up on Rick. More often than not, they found him fully dressed but sound asleep sprawled across the top of the linens on the bed.

Sue sent her husband a letter of encouragement. She told him that she and the boys were behind him—believed in him. She knew, she wrote, that he would be a big success in San Antonio. Before long, Sue secured a job as an industry market revenue analyst with responsibility for balance sheet, budget and plan preparation in the San Antonio office of Southwestern Bell.

With 1-year-old Timmy perched on her hip, Sue supervised the relocation of the household. The moving van picked up the furniture and all of the big boxes.

Ann and Kirsten were at the house helping Sue pull together all the small stuff to load in the car for the trip down. Throughout this process, Sue handed off items to Ann to deliver to others in the area.

Everything was packed up. Everyone was ready to go. Unfortunately, the car Ann came in was locked. And the keys were in the ignition.

After a call to AAA, Sue went to her freezer and emerged with a pitcher of frozen margaritas—a concoction she learned to love during the time she worked in Texas. The other women were impressed—all packed up and still Sue had what she needed to put together an impromptu party.

The women sat on the porch sipping their drinks. Two hours later, after sharing a margarita with the AAA guy, the car was unlocked, the keys retrieved and Sue's merry little band of boys was on its way to San Antonio—a city with a reputation for using any and every excuse to throw a party.

7

The McFarlands chose a home with an open floor plan and a natural circular flow perfect for entertaining—the right match for a woman who loved to throw parties. It was situated in Terrell Hills, a suburban community just off Austin Highway in Central Bexar County. Five miles northeast of downtown San Antonio, Terrell Hills was a 1.2-square-mile island in the ocean of a major metropolitan area.

The town adopted a home rule charter in 1957 to keep from being annexed and washed into the multicultural sea of the larger city, where more than 55 percent of the population was Hispanic. Terrell Hills—87 percent Anglo—was, like neighboring Alamo Heights, an enclave of yuppie sensibilities that cherished its separate identity. The two towns also shared a prestigious zip code—78209—and the residents labeled as 09'ers. If you lived there, you carried that badge with pride. If you didn't, calling someone as 09'er was an insult whose intensity varied from speaker to speaker, from comic condescension to disdainful loathing.

It was a leafy green community of good schools, chi-chi boutiques and extravagant grocery stores. It was a great place to drive an SUV and raise a family.

In this comfortable middle-class backdrop of normalcy, the McFarland family settled into their new home at 351 Arcadia Place. From the first day, though, it was apparent to neighbors that for this family, normal was only a façade.

The weekend of the move, the family in the house behind

them—Carrie and Steve Miller and their three children, Billy, Stephanie and Wesley—were away at Lake LBJ for the weekend. When they returned home, Steve looked in the backyard. He recognized change at first, but not the source of it. Then his eyes zeroed in on the fresh stump sticking out of the ground where a hackberry tree used to be. He went outside for a closer examination. His first thought was that an engineer had ordered it cut because it interfered with the power lines. But when he called the government offices of Terrell Hills, they denied responsibility.

Puzzled, he looked out the window again. On the other side of the fence, he saw his new neighbor, Rick McFarland, holding his youngest son, Timmy. He went back out and introduced himself over the fence. After they shared a few pleasantries, Steve asked, "Rick, did you see our tree? It was here on Friday."

Rick shrugged.

"Did you see it walk off?"

"No," Rick said.

Steve was amazed—Rick answered the question as if Steve had serious concerns that the tree had grown legs and moved on to another yard. Did the man have any sense of humor? Steve took a more direct approach. "Did you see anyone come into my yard and cut down my tree?"

"No."

"Rick, did you cut down my tree?"

"Yes."

"Why, Rick, why?"

"The tree was dropping too many leaves in my yard."

Dumbfounded, Steve looked in the McFarland yard and saw that the only leaves that fell from his tree landed in the graveled dog run along the fence. "That was my tree. It was in my yard. I know you're a Yankee, but down here you come on somebody's property and you're lucky to make it to the property line alive. What were you thinking?"

"I'll make it up to you," Rick said.

"How?"

"Do you have a website?"

"No."

"I'll design a website for you."

Steve thought the offer was odd—and Rick was odder still. He didn't think about it again until a couple of weeks later when he heard back from Rick. "I'm almost finished with the website design. It'll cost you twenty-five hundred dollars."

"Twenty-five hundred dollars? I thought you were doing it for free. I thought you did it in exchange for cutting down my tree. Twenty-five hundred dollars? Forget it."

"I can't. I already registered the domain name."

"Shove it, Rick."

Not exactly an auspicious beginning for building new neighborly relations.

Steve told a friend the story of the hackberry tree and the website a while later. His friend said, "That's bizarre. What's that guy's name?"

"Rick McFarland."

"Rick McFarland? That crook? He came by my office to sell me advertising to go on the side of a VIA bus. We went back and forth about it and McFarland didn't want to take no for an answer. But the bottom line was, I didn't need advertising on the side of a bus and I told him so. A few days later, I get a call from McFarland's boss. He called to personally thank me for the major contract I had signed. I told him, 'I didn't sign a contract with anybody. If you have a contract with my signature on it, it is a forgery.' "

So much for Rick's first job in San Antonio, selling bus advertising for Transportation Display. Rick then spent seven months with Clear Blue Media in Internet advertising sales. After June 2000, he was occupied in dubious self-employment schemes and caring for his boys.

8

The hackberry tree was not the only bone of contention the Millers had with their new neighbors. There was also the matter of Sally, the McFarlands' dog. Typically, Sally stayed by the back fence in a small graveled dog run—Rick called it a "corral"—except when the boys played with her in the open yard.

Sally barked all the time, day and night. It was driving Steve nuts and keeping him awake at night. One fall day, he was walking around the block. As he passed the McFarland front yard, he spotted Rick. They shared some small talk, then Steve asked, "Do you ever hear dogs barking at night?"

"No."

"I know it's in the neighborhood. It sounds like it's coming from here on Arcadia. Have you heard it?" Steve asked again.

"No. No."

Steve was stunned that Rick was denying this, and tried to push his buttons a bit more. "If I find that dog, I'll give him some alum water."

"What does that do?" Rick asked.

"It closes up your throat."

"How does it work?"

"I don't know, but we used to do it as a fraternity prank in college."

"Really." Rick said. "And they couldn't talk? Where can you get it?"

"I don't know—that was a long time ago. A drug store or someplace like that."

Rick continued on with this line of questioning about the alum—demonstrating what Steve thought a rather curious and disturbing interest.

Next door to the McFarlands, Charlene Schooling was also concerned about Sally. A devoted dog lover—and owner of seven of them—Charlene was more bothered by Sally being left outside all the time than she was by the barking. She asked Rick why he never allowed the dog in.

"Because she chewed on a rug and Susan wasn't happy."

"Why don't you give her rawhide to chew on?"

"I'm afraid if I give her a bone to chew on it will teach her to chew, and she'll chew up everything in the house."

Despite Rick's casting of blame on his wife, Charlene soon noticed that whenever Rick was out of town, Sally was inside. She slept on the floor of Sue's bedroom every one of those nights. Sue loved that dog. In fact, she was the one who'd named her Sally. Sue wanted a little girl whom she could name Sarah and call Sally. Instead she had three boys, but found a way to put the name to good use.

Sue also named the gray-and-white family cat they'd brought with them from St. Louis—he was called Marvin. When Charlene asked about the unusual appellation for a cat, Sue said it was her husband's middle name. "I had to name the cat that to make sure I would not have to name one of our kids Marvin."

Sue worked a lot and was not around much, but, eventually, the Millers met her, too. Their boys brought them together. Carrie thought the McFarland kids were so cute and diminutive—they reminded her of characters from Whoville. At first, she was put off by Sue's abrasive Midwestern mannerisms, but in time she was able to see past that non-Southern façade and learn that Sue was friendly, personable and easy to be around.

Carrie's son Wesley played with William a lot. He loved

to go over to the McFarlands' and jump on their trampoline. Carrie never felt comfortable, though, with her son being over there when Susan was not home. Something about Rick gave her a mild case of the creeps, though she didn't understand why. She did know that when the McFarland boys were around Rick, they screamed, ran wild and demonstrated no manners at all. When they were with Susan alone, they were still boisterous boys, but much more calm, at ease and polite.

Wesley Miller went to James' sixth birthday party in September 1999. His dad, Steve, was at home watching a Dallas Cowboys football game. When the phone rang, he let the answering machine pick up. "Steve, this is Rick McFarland. Could you come over here and see if Wesley will play nicer with other children?"

Steve ignored the message. He put up with Rick's kids climbing over his fence and acting up in his home. It was pay-back for Rick, Steve thought.

The phone rang again. "Steve, this is Rick McFarland again. I was wondering if you could come over and pick Wesley up? He's not playing well with other children."

Rick's own kids didn't play well around Rick, Steve thought, why should Wesley be any different?

Again, the phone rang. "Steve, this is Rick McFarland again. The party is almost over . . ."

The football game was, too. Steve walked around to the McFarlands' and retrieved Wesley.

The Millers were not the only ones to notice Rick's problems with the boys. Melissa St. John, William's swim coach in the summer of 2000, observed that Rick did not seem to have control over his sons' behavior. When they acted out, he was incapable of normalizing the situation.

Although only William was on the Wave swim team that year, Rick brought along Timmy and James. In and of itself, their presence was not an uncommon practice. However, unlike other parents who brought their children along, Rick seemed unaware of his responsibility to keep his children under control. Staff spoke to him about the need for constant supervision on more than one occasion.

At swim meets, the coaching staff soon learned that Rick was not a good volunteer judge, either. His failure to respond to situations in the pool in a timely manner caused other parents to complain. The coaches tried to place him in a remote spot where problems were less likely to arise.

Rick tried hard to fit in, but despite his best efforts, his lack of social skills always seemed to leave him looking in from the outside. After spending an evening at a Town Club party at the San Antonio Country Club with Bill and Molly Matthews, Rick longed to be a member of the exclusive organization. He felt that belonging to this group would bolster his image in the community and boost his own sense of self-worth.

Rick bugged Bill to put him and Susan up for membership. It was not a simple matter of submitting a request. Bill would have had to mount an aggressive campaign to find other members willing to write letters of sponsorship as well. Bill told his wife it would be a waste of time— everybody already knew how weird Rick was.

Rick was determined. He called several times wanting a copy of the membership directory to launch an appeal on his own. Bill was reluctant to cooperate. But one night, while Molly visited with Sue, Rick went over to the Matthewses' home. He sat down with Bill and looked through the list of names. His effort was stillborn since Bill did not devote any energy to it, and Rick was devastated by the disappointment. Sue, on the other hand was indifferent. She just shrugged and said, "It's more Rick's kind of thing than mine."

One day, Harriet and Ned Wells would play a pivotal role in the unfolding McFarland mystery. Their initial contacts with their across-the-street neighbors, however, were odd, but unremarkable. The first family member they met was 8-year-old William. One Sunday afternoon, he crossed the street and walked into their home without knocking.

He offered to sweep their sidewalk for one dollar. Harriet agreed and three minutes later, the doorbell rang. William said that he had finished the job. Harriet could see that there was still a lot of debris on the walk, but he was just a little kid, so she gave him a couple of bucks and sent him on his way.

Next, the Wellses met Sue in her front yard and thought she was absolutely delightful. Ned and Harriet invited her over for lunch. When Sue left, she still had their wineglass in her hand. She returned a few minutes later full of smiles and apologies—that glass now has a place of honor in the Wellses' new home.

It was not unusual to see William mowing the family's yard at a time when Harriet thought he was too small to operate the machinery. She also saw him in the Wells' front yard playing entrepreneur. The first time she saw him she asked him why.

"I want to buy a Palm Pilot."

Harriet thought that was an odd desire for an 8-year-old.

The Wellses never understood why William always set up the table on their side of the street, but assumed it was at Rick's instigation. Time and again, they watched this scenario with a combination of annoyance and curiosity.

Then one weekend, Harriet and Ned returned from an out-of-town trip to discover Rick and William sitting at a card table in the Wellses' front yard selling something to people in the passing cars. They already had concluded that Rick was weird, and decided to ignore him rather than create a scene.

After dark that evening, William was out there alone. When Harriet noticed he was running out in the street to stop cars, she knew she had to intervene. She told William it was time to go home. That was the last time their front yard was used for a makeshift store.

Harriet and Ned would have liked to have more contact with Sue, but they could not tolerate Rick, and avoided building a closer relationship. For the life of them, they could not figure out why the two were together.

They also wondered if Rick was capable of speaking to his boys in a normal tone of voice. The sound of his screaming drifted across Arcadia Place day after day.

At work, Sue received another promotion into the Southwestern Bell Telephone finance operations group. She did not work out of the location most people in San Antonio associate with the company. That elegant structure with its sweeping broad stairway that slid down to a lush, green, serene section of the famed Riverwalk was the corporate headquarters.

Her office was in the plain tan building at the corner of St. Mary's and McCullough. It was on the river but not a scenic section of it. A walk across the parking lot led to a fence that overlooked the water. Below, the river was brown and sluggish. Its borders blighted with scraggly weeds and abandoned concrete ramps. It offered no sidewalks or any other enticement to exploration for any but the most intrepid urban naturalist.

Sue reached her office by ascending to the eleventh floor and wending her way through a rabbit warren of endless monotonous cubicles to a corner work area with one tall, narrow window. The drab atmosphere was brightened by pictures of William, James and Timmy at school or at Disney World and with Mother's Day gifts crafted by the three biggest loves of her life.

From this unassuming space, Sue oversaw the general ledger accounting for this division of the corporation. Her staff included three managers and five administrative support staff.

Their monthly routine was rigid and repetitive. The first week of every month was the time when the heat under the pressure cooker was set on high. Everyone worked longer hours to close out the books for the preceding month. Then they prepared financial reports for the corporate office. Sue was key in this process.

This week was grueling every month, but in April, July,

October and January the intensity was even higher as quarterly report requirements added to the workload.

Sue was responsible for making adjustments and reconciling hundreds of accounts in Arkansas, Missouri, Kansas, Texas and Oklahoma. She pored over them looking for any odd entry and investigating its origin and the appropriateness of its classification. No detail, no entry was too small.

The last week of the month resembled what most people would regard as a normal work week. Sue followed up on the reconciliation and did as much advance work as possible for the closing week ahead.

Then the cycle began anew. Despite the burdensome workload in a corporate downsizing environment, despite the stifling sameness of one beige cubicle wall after another, the emotional lives of the folks on the eleventh floor intertwined, and tight bonds formed. Southwestern Bell fostered a family-oriented atmosphere and encouraged community involvement. Junior Achievement—where Sue was an active volunteer—brought business professionals into the school to teach children about commerce and free enterprise. This organization ranked high in SBC's favor.

The women in Sue's area of the floor were a close-knit group who socialized often outside of the workplace. They lunched together often, had frequent evening get-togethers, from book clubs to Mary Kay parties, and during the holidays, they participated in a Christmas cookie exchange.

Sue was devoted to Southwestern Bell and it showed in her excellent performance. She thrived in the professional environment and pursued advancement when the opportunities arose. Nonetheless, in this workplace full of bean counters, Sue did not fit the mold. For most people on the eleventh floor, the stereotype held true—they were quiet, introverted number-wonks. Sue livened up the floor with her outgoing personality and her sudden silence-bursting explosions of laughter.

If Sue received a promotion outside of this division, her

presence would have been sorely missed. When she did leave, the reason for her departure landed like a sledgehammer on glass—leaving shattered productivity and shards of pain.

9

By 1999, Rick was involved with the Promise Keepers, an organization that championed the institutions of fatherhood and traditional marriage through the principles of love, protection and biblical values. He received his personalized certificate of commitment in which he promised to be obedient to the "Great Commandment" in the book of Mark: "And thou shalt love the Lord thy God with all thy heart, and with all thy soul, and with all thy mind, and with all thy strength; this is the first commandment. And the second is like, namely this, Thou shalt love thy neighbor as thyself. There is none other commandment greater than these."

He also committed to the "Great Commission" in Matthew: "Go ye therefore, and teach all nations, baptizing them in the name of the Father, and of the Son and of the Holy Ghost: Teaching them to observe all things whatsoever I have commanded you: and, lo, I am with you always, even unto the end of the world."

In August, Rick volunteered to work at the San Antonio Men's Conference at the Alamodome. Tens of thousands of men gathered to hear messages of salvation, holiness and purity, stewardship, disciplines, family, unity and revival. The thank-you note Rick received after the gathering read: "You, as a volunteer, make the conferences possible through your labor and ministry. We praise God that he prepared you and raised you up to serve Him. For the Promise Keepers staff—thank you and may God, our Father, richly bless you."

Bill Matthews' dislike of Rick McFarland was shared by the spouses of many of Sue's friends. They were surprised and not a bit entertained when Rick talked for hours about Pokemon cards. They were annoyed at his habit of "face-talking"—always up in their faces, violating their personal space.

Bill knew Sue thought Rick was a computer whiz, but being in the computer business himself, he realized Rick was just an amateur with no depth of knowledge. Like a lot of men, many husbands of Sue's friends were uncomfortable with Rick's atypical role in the family. They squirmed at Sue's apparent domination of Rick. But they assumed Rick liked to be bossed around by his wife—that for the McFarlands, this lop-sided relationship worked.

Sue's women friends, for the most part, wrote Rick off as a nerd and a gadget person—the guy who ran around with the video camera at all the family get-togethers. As a rule, they tolerated as much of him as necessary to maintain their friendship with Sue. More often than not, the women got together without their spouses.

Once Sue had moved to San Antonio, she and Sandy coordinated their summer and holiday trips to visit family in St. Louis to ensure that they would both be there at the same time. The bonds they nurtured would serve them well when tragedy struck.

In 2000, Sandy's world fell to pieces at her feet. Her second child, and first son, was born with Down syndrome—a daunting challenge for any parent. Then, when he was just 4 months old, Sandy had to endure the agony of waiting in the sterile environs of a hospital while the tiny baby underwent open-heart surgery.

Nearly depleted by this chain of events, Sandy took another blow. One month after her son's surgery, she was diagnosed with breast cancer. Through it all, she turned to Sue for strength, comfort and understanding. Sue, although she felt helpless by the distance that kept them apart, was supportive and uplifting. She told Sandy that if she wanted her there for her chemotherapy, she would drop everything and come. "If you need me just to hold your hair while you're puking in the toilet, I'm there."

Sue was happy to offer support to her friend—she was just frustrated that she could not seem to do the same for her husband. In fact, since they'd moved to San Antonio, he seemed to be spiraling out of control.

Sue discovered that Rick kept a telephone from a former job and used the number to charge up several thousand dollars' worth of calls. Sue told her sister Ann, "He's done another unethical thing and it's going to cost me a fortune to get him out of it. I'm going to divorce him. I swear I'll divorce him."

Her extreme distress over the situation kept the two sisters on the phone for a very long time.

Rick felt discomfort in the relationship, too. In the fall of 2000, excruciating headaches drove him to the emergency room seeking relief. When asked about any medications, he told the doctor he was taking some of his children's Adderol because of the problems he was having with concentration and attention. Rick theorized that if he did not feel any different, he did not have ADD. To the contrary, he found he could concentrate better when he took the drug. The emergency room physician believed the headaches could be secondary to his Adderol use and discouraged him from continuing with his self medication.

The Wednesday night before Thanksgiving in 2000, Sue's former sister-in-law Debbie and her family drove from Houston to San Marcos. There at Southwest Texas State University, they picked up Debbie's oldest son and headed down Interstate Highway 35 to San Antonio and the McFarland home.

Thanksgiving morning, Sue and Debbie hustled the kids and menfolk out of the house to the mall and a movie as they tackled the holiday meal preparation. Experience in a number of cooking classes gave Sue a flair in her cooking and presentation. Debbie enjoyed trying out new recipes with her and preparing special desserts for the neighbors who would join them after dinner.

The next day, Debbie and Sue got up before dawn to hit the Thanksgiving sales. They returned with a car full of packages and prepared breakfast for the two families. Then they all went down to the Riverwalk to enjoy the holiday festivities. It was a wonderful time for all—they would repeat it in 2001.

A couple of months later, recently divorced Kirsten asked Sue about her plans to end the marriage.

"We're going to work on this—we'll work it out," Sue said. "We're going to be partners to raise these boys. Not like a real marriage—a partnership."

Kirsten, who had been there and done that, said, "You'll get to the point when divorce feels right and then you will do it *for* the kids."

Sue said, "Rick said his religion forbids divorce, and he won't let it happen."

10

The marriage of Rick and Sue McFarland never sailed on halcyon seas. In attempts to rehabilitate the relationship and perhaps resuscitate feelings of love and devotion, they took their troubles to counselors when they lived in the St. Louis area and again after they moved to San Antonio.

The couple had many obstacles to success. One was the negative attitude Rick's parents had toward Sue. But worst of all, whenever they passed judgment on her, Rick did not come to her defense—he always sided with his parents.

With her strong work ethic, Sue chafed under the frustrations created by Rick's sporadic employment record as his contribution to the family finances devolved into home business schemes. Rick became a stay-at-home dad and, like both of his brothers, his wife was the main breadwinner for the household.

One of the reasons for Rick's failure in the workplace was his method for choosing positions. He did not look for work that he loved, he tried to find jobs that fit the persona he wanted to create.

He enjoyed tinkering with computers and, in all likelihood, would have found fulfillment in that area of employment. But it simply did not fit into the self-image he envisioned. So instead he chose to work in sales, where he was handicapped by his stutter and lack of social skills.

In San Antonio, he started an on-line business, DOT-NETA, a company that paid cash to investors holding notes

on loans for cars, life insurance, real estate and mobile homes.
The original investor had the advantage of cash in hand and
DOTNETA reaped the profits from the long-term interest.
At least that was the plan, but Rick did not seem capable of
fulfilling the promise in a tangible way.

In both 2000 and 2001, Rick told Sue that he earned about
$20,000 each year—a fraction of Sue's salary at Southwest-
ern Bell. Sue dutifully reported this money on her tax return
and paid the taxes on it. But she sure could not figure out
where or how Rick made any money.

To complicate matters, her boys all had behavioral problems requiring medication. She wondered if the boys' emotional health was worsened by Rick's inconsistent child care.

The combination of these shortcomings made Susan con-
template divorce on many occasions. Whenever she considered the possibility, she made journal entries to document
her grievances. The first one was dated on her forty-second
birthday—December 31, 2000.[2]

> I am so angry. I just found out that Rick had made a
> decision about the prescriptions taken by James and
> William without consulting me or the boys' doctor.
> Four days earlier, on the advice of his sister-in-law,
> Debbie, Rick and his parents decided to give the boys
> "a vacation" from their medication. Rick left the pills
> at his parents' house when he drove back to rejoin me
> at my mother's.
>
> I fumed as I drove straight over to Rick's parents'
> and retrieved the Wellbutrin and Prozac that William
> was supposed to take every day. I chastised Rick for
> not talking to me before taking action and for putting
> William's health at risk. He shrugged off my concerns.
>
> On New Year's Day, as we drove from St. Louis
> back to San Antonio, I asked Rick: "Did you give
> William his pills before we left?"

[2] Sue's journal excerpts have been edited for clarity and continuity.

Rick blew up. "You packed the boys' bags," he told me. "That means you were responsible for the pills. Besides, the boys were doing well without any medications."

As the argument continued, he repeated that assertion again and again. I knew he was wrong.

The next day, I went back to work and the boys went back to school. William came home on the school bus, but Rick was supposed to pick Timmy up from school no later than 5:30.

At 5:50, I was sitting at my desk at Southwestern Bell trying to catch up on the work that piled up while I was out of town, when the phone rang. It was Kathy, the secretary at Timmy's school. "Timmy is still here," she told me. "I called your home phone, your husband's car phone and his business line and got no answer."

I couldn't leave work yet and I couldn't count on Rick, so I called our friends, Doug and Margot Cromack. They agreed to pick up Timmy, so I called Terry, the director of the school, and let her know who was on the way.

At 6:30, my phone rang again. This time it was Rick. "I'm on my way to pick up Timmy," he said.

I was mad at him and I told him so. Instead of apologizing, he just complained that he could not understand why no one contacted him. When I told them the school tried, he paid no attention.

Rick's obsession with shopping is growing out of control. On January 9, he was out so late, he fought my efforts to get him out of bed before I went to work.

"It's raining," he said. "I can run late because I'll be driving the boys to school."

"Please get up and get going," I begged him before I left for work at 7:30.

"Don't worry. I want to go a little late to miss the traffic mess."

After work, I picked Timmy up at school and no-ticed he did not have a lunch box. When I asked Rick about it, he blamed me for not checking Timmy's classroom thoroughly.

Later that night, I asked him when the kids did get to school that day.

"Noon," he said.

I was flabbergasted and demanded to know why they got there so late in the day.

"They were watching educational TV and I saw no reason to interrupt their learning," he said. "Besides, I had to get them to pick up toys and lift furniture so that I could remove the rug from their room."

Did he think these were good reasons? Was he re-ally that clueless?

The next day, I got a call from Timmy's teacher, Miss Noelle. "Today," she told me, "Timmy did not get to school until 10. And both today and yesterday, he had bad behavior days." She went on to remind me that Martha, the assistant director of the school, had told Rick more than once that the school handbook was quite clear—kids must be there by 9. She then added, "Timmy needs a strict routine."

I knew that but Rick didn't seem to. I promised to talk to Rick.

Earlier that day, Rick had called and said that I needed to watch Timmy that evening because he needed to take William and James down the street to Indian Guides.

"I have an appointment to have my hair cut and colored at 5 and won't be home until 7 or 7:30," I re-minded him. "You need to find someone to watch Timmy until I get home."

I called from the hair salon to find out where I needed to pick up Timmy but got no answer on the home phone or on the cell. I went home hoping to find an answer there. William and James were home—in William's room with the door shut playing video

*games where they could not hear the phone. They
never went to Indian Guides. Rick had gone shopping
again and took Timmy with him.*

*Our house was filled with Rick's purchases. He
bought multiples of anything that he thought was a
good deal or came with a rebate. On Saturday, I
asked him not to buy anything else until he had returned all the stuff he had accumulated. He seemed to
agree with my request. I was concerned that he would
lose track and not return or rebate the items in time.*

"But I have 90 days to return the stuff," he insisted.

*"Rick," I said, "we get the credit card bill in thirty
days. If it's not returned by then, we have to pay the
interest."*

*He had been out several evenings this past week re-
turning purchases so I thought he would not be out
too long that night. But at midnight, he still wasn't
home—how could these returns be so time-consuming?
I called and asked him where he was and what he
could possibly be returning at this hour.*

*"I'm at Wal-Mart wandering the aisles and explor-
ing possibilities," he said.*

*The next morning, he could not get up. He said he
was "sick." I think he was worn out from his glut of
shopping at all hours. He finally rose at 11. To my
dismay, he unloaded more purchases from the car—
tons of reorganizing supplies for the stair closet, more
than could possibly fit in there.*

*At 3, he left home to pick up the boys from the
youth symphony. He took them with him to return
some of the "good deals" he had picked up since
Thanksgiving. He didn't get home until 10:30 that
night—far too late for a school night.*

*On Monday, January 15, I got home from work
at 7:15. The house was a mess. Dirty dishes were
scattered throughout the kitchen, the contents of the
stair closet were strewn about the living room and
shopping bags were everywhere. There were at least*

twenty new bags from Wal-Mart. Rick bought a bunch
of kitchen items including replacements for all the
kids' dishes and our coffee mugs and an assortment
of wrought iron accessories—three or four of each
item. He had also purchased a cheap office chair for
William and gave it to him to assemble.

"There's nothing wrong with what we were using,
Rick," I told him. "I don't want to replace it all with
cheap stuff you picked up at Wal-Mart on a whim."

Later that evening, I was organizing my home desk
and ran across a fanny pack. In it, I found a huge wad
of receipts. I leafed through them and found an email
exchange between Rick and Office Depot. The store
was complaining about Rick's attempts to make voluminous returns—often bringing back items with a
hole in the packaging making it apparent that he had
already sent in for the rebate. These returns, they
wrote, were a violation of store policy. One Office Depot receipt in the pack, dated two days earlier, indicated that he had returned so many items that he had
enough credit to purchase two $250 Palm Pilots. I
was beginning to understand why the returns were
consuming so much of his time.

I asked Rick, "Why did you buy these Palm Pilots?"

"I'm going to rebate them," he said.

"What are you going to do with two of them?"

"I'm going to upgrade William's Vista Organizer."

He still wasn't answering my question. That was it.
I gave him an ultimatum: "Either you return everything or I am filing a divorce today. Mentally, you are
losing it, Rick. Totally losing it."

The next morning, in the middle of dressing the
boys and getting them off to school, Rick sat down to
watch an infomercial about a new treatment for focus-
ing. "It might be good for me and William," he said
and insisted I watch it.

I did for several minutes and decided it was worth-

less and possibly dangerous. "You are not to give that treatment to William," I ordered before I left for work.

It was a long day at the office. I called Rick around 6:30 to find out where he and the boys were. He said they were eating at McDonald's.

"There's plenty of food at home. Why are you eating at McDonald's?"

"Because," was all he said.

"Have the boys finished their homework?"

"Almost—William has a little more to complete."

"When will you be home, Rick?"

"In about an hour," he said.

I went home at 8 to see the boys before they went to bed. But when I arrived, the house was empty. They didn't get back home from Wal-Mart until 10 P.M. When they did straggle in, the boys were arguing with each other.

Apparently, William—my nine-year-old with Attention Deficit Disorder—had been put in charge of watching Timmy in the video section while Rick completed returns at the front desk. It was no surprise to me that William lost track of Timmy after a while. But both William and James were in trouble with their dad for letting their little brother get lost. Because of that, incessant squabbling had erupted between the kids.

We all woke up a little late the next morning. I helped dress the boys so that Rick could get them to school in time. Of course, when they left, homework assignments were not complete.

On Friday of that week, I got home at 5:40 but our youngest son was not there. "Where's Timmy?" I asked Rick.

"I emailed you and told you to pick him up," Rick accused.

"I did not get an email."

"You must have missed it," he insisted.

I went to pick up Timmy but the next Monday morning, I made it a point to double-check my email box. Nothing from Rick. Once again, he had failed to pick up Timmy before 5:30 and once again he shifted the blame to someone else.

Saturday evening, Rick talked on the phone with William's teacher, Miss Griffin, for almost an hour. Rick told me that they talked about the difficult time William was having on his ADD medicine holiday.

"Why is William on a holiday?" I asked.

Rick went on the defensive, making arguments that made no sense, but the bottom line was, that without my knowledge, William had not had his ADD medicine since Christmas break.

On Sunday morning, I got up before 7 with Timmy and James. After I fixed their breakfast, they piled on top of me on the sofa and watched a movie. I read about the presidential inauguration in the newspaper.

After the movie was over, I rearranged the art in the living room and cleaned up the kitchen. Around 10, I woke up Rick. "I'm tired. Get up and watch the kids. I want to take a nap after getting up with the boys at dawn."

Rick was angered by this request and I had to drag him out of bed. I slept until 1 in the afternoon when the boys came and bounced on my bed.

When I went downstairs, the family room was in total disarray. Rick sneered at me and said, "Now, I'm taking a nap since you made me get up."

"What have you been doing since you got up?" I asked.

"I watched two movies with the kids."

"It's after 1 and the leaves still have not been blown or raked."

"I'll get to it in the next few days. If that's a problem for you, you can blow them yourself."

"Since you have no income, the least you can do is

*the yard work without constantly being reminded," I
snapped.*

*He ignored me, went upstairs and went to bed.
When he got up, he hassled me about the clean-up I
had done. I had to explain each and every item I put
in the giveaway or pitch piles. He salvaged useless
things from both categories.*

*On Saturday, January 27, Rick spent the entire day
volunteering at the rodeo. Before he left home, I asked
him to be home by 6 since we were having guests for
dinner. Instead he got home at 7—he just had to go
shopping at North Star Mall when he left his volunteer job at the Coliseum.*

*The next morning, Rick was out in the garage for a
long time. I asked him what he was up to.*

*"I went to Dillard's at North Star Mall last night
and found four scooters for $25 apiece. I'm exchang-
ing the handlebars and wheelie bars on the new ones
for the beat up ones on the kids' scooters. But it's not
going to cost any money because I am returning the
new scooters with the old parts to Dillards."*

*"Dillards is very picky about returns," I warned
him.*

"I'm not worried. I can handle it," he assured me.

*I am becoming very concerned about Rick's spend-
ing habits. He has not posted any activity to the
Quicken account since November. He gave a lame excuse about no longer being able to download transac-
tions from 2000, but other folks at work have Quicken
Visas and have not had download problems. I am
afraid he is lying to me and has racked up so many
purchases that he knows I will get mad if I see that.*

*Later that day, I was disposing of the Adderol that
neither William nor James take any longer. Rick
stopped me and said not to get rid of it because he
was giving it to Timmy.*

*Giving it to Timmy? He had never cleared this with
me or with Dr. Martin. He just began his own experi-
ment. "You know how I feel about you doing this sort
of thing without my knowledge or consent."*

*"I don't need your permission on everything," he
snapped back.*

*On Monday, Rick called me at work. "I phoned the
General Manager at Dillard's and he said that I can
return the scooters without a problem. But, maybe, we
should call around and see if any of our friends want
to buy them since they are such a good deal."*

*"Why don't you spend the afternoon blowing
leaves instead of acting like a personal shopper for
our friends?"*

"Okay. I promise I'll return the scooters today."

*At 5:20, I called Rick and told him that I was pick-
ing up Timmy. We got home at 6. Rick was working on
homework with William. By the time I picked up the
house and made dinner, Rick had fallen asleep. The
boys and I ate together and watched a movie.*

*At 8, Rick got up and said he was going to Dil-
lard's. He crawled into bed at midnight that night letting me know that he also spent time at Target.*

Susan's journal entries stopped here on January 29, 2001,
and did not resume for sixteen months. Had the situation in
the household improved? Or did she just decide to tough it
out because an attorney advised her that since Rick had been
staying home caring for the boys, he would probably get
custody?

11

Despite Rick's flaws as a parent, the staff at Woodridge Elementary, where William and James attended school, saw him as an involved father. He stood out among the parents of the 900 other students for his willingness to participate.

He volunteered to help teachers with writing workshops and other activities. He came to all the children's programs from string recitals to Christmas pageants. He attended every school meeting and never missed a summer placement consultation for his boys. He demonstrated the care, concern and love for his sons that educators wanted to see. No one noticed that he was a bit stranger than the average parent.

One spring day in 2001, Charlene spotted Rick McFarland pacing back and forth in his front yard in an obvious state of excitement. He was dressed in navy blue Bermuda shorts, a Henley shirt, a pair of cowboy boots and a cowboy hat. His outfit was comical but his behavior even more so. He bounced around the yard and peered up the street with all the exuberance of a child awaiting Santa's imminent arrival.

For hours, Charlene made sporadic checks out her window and there was Rick, still keeping vigil. Finally, he was rewarded. Rick's parents, Mona and Dick, pulled up in front of his home. His outfit and his irrepressible anticipation were all because his parents were coming. How odd.

• • •

By the summer of 2001, it was apparent that all was not well at 351 Arcadia. For some time, swim coach Melissa St. John recognized the chaos that swirled around the McFarland boys whenever she saw them with their father. She knew William was intimidated by his dad. She felt Rick pushed his oldest son to excel in areas where William's only possible response was frustration and failure. But she knew James adored his father, wrapping his arms around him at every opportunity.

One day at swim class, Melissa noticed several small, dark, circular contusions on William's face. She asked what happened.

He said that his dad wanted to teach him a lesson because he had not been paying attention during his tennis class. So Dad slammed tennis balls at him while making him stand motionless on the court.

Melissa was horrified, but a niggling doubt about the accuracy of the story wiggled in her head—William had lied to her about less important things before. But she looked at the face of the loving and creative boy and she knew what she saw was unusual and not consistent with a fall or with running into something. She said that his dad was wrong to do that and she would call his mother.

William didn't think it would do any good.

After talking it over with another coach and her supervisor, Melissa decided to report the incident to Child Protective Services (CPS). She hoped to remain nameless but was informed that CPS does not act on the basis of an anonymous report.

Reluctantly, she identified herself and asked if it would be appropriate for her to talk to Mrs. McFarland to make sure that William would not face disciplinary action for speaking to her. CPS told her that it was her decision to make.

Melissa then called Sue McFarland and told her what William had said and informed her about the call to CPS.

Sue doubted William's story and never saw the marks on his face.

Melissa insisted that she knew what she saw and that the bruises were not fresh.

Sue dropped her initial disbelief and admitted her sense of helplessness to change the situation. She was powerless, she said, to make Rick take his prescription for his obsessive-compulsive disorder and ineffective in overcoming Rick's objections to getting treatment for their son.

Melissa urged Sue to get help for William right away—once they get to a certain age, she said, you can't reach them. You have a limited window of time. She also related other problems that had risen with the boys during swim practice and added that Rick knew about all these things but did not seem to care.

Sue was angry that Rick never mentioned any of them to her. She didn't ask him to do much more than take the children where they needed to go, she said. She could not keep babysitters because they did not like being around Rick and she was afraid to leave him because she worried about possible joint custody, she added.

She had tried counseling, she said, but each one of the professionals gave up when Rick would not take his medicine or follow their therapeutic advice.

The conversation ended on a brighter note. Melissa invited William to attend her art class that fall at First Presbyterian Church.

"I'll make every effort to have him there."

Later that day, Rick called Melissa and accused her of causing problems for him with his wife.

Melissa explained that she had a legal and moral obligation to file the report. She then emphasized the need for William to have consistency and focus in his day-to-day life.

That angered Rick even more. Although he did not deny lobbing tennis balls at William, he insisted that she should have reported this to him first.

Melissa told him that he would have to settle the matter with CPS and then she hung up.

The next practice day, William confronted his coach about turning in his dad. Melissa urged William to think about what he would do if the roles were reversed—if he were the adult. After giving it some thought, William agreed that she had done the right thing.

Soon, Rick was up in Melissa's face, crowding her personal space although he spoke in a soft voice. Threat bubbled below the surface as he questioned her justification for causing him so much grief.

Melissa did not back down. She reiterated her belief that she was obligated to report the situation to the authorities. She added that she wouldn't hesitate to do it again if it was necessary. Then she turned and walked away.

Melissa was now concerned about her personal safety and asked her staff and select male parents to keep an eye on Mr. McFarland when he was in the pool complex. She also told her assistant coaches to let her know of questionable markings on William's body in the future.

At the end of the week, William approached his coach again. "I made a mistake about what I said. I just had an accident. I tripped and fell into the sharp place on the tennis ball machine."

"Did you do that a bunch of times to get all of those bruises?" she asked.

"I don't know," was all William could say.

Sue attended swim practice more often and Rick seemed more attentive to his children. Melissa assumed CPS was providing the necessary intervention. It was an assumption she would later regret.

12

Susan went to St. Louis with her husband and her boys that July. After a few days, she returned to home and work. The rest of the family stayed in Missouri for a four-week visit. She was alone in her home with Sally the dog and Marvin the cat.

Next door, in the wee hours of the night, Susan Schooling was deep in thought, still awake. A woman's "blood-curdling scream" ripped her from her reverie. She bolted to her feet and ran to her mother, Charlene.

Charlene maintained that Susan must have been dreaming. Susan insisted that she was awake and it sounded as if someone discovered an intruder with knife in hand.

The next night, Charlene and Susan were concerned as the hours passed and Sue had not returned home from work. When 9:30—Sue's normal bedtime—came and went, Susan was alarmed. The memory of the scream from the night before made her imagination dwell on the worst possibilities.

At 10:30, Sue pulled into her driveway. Susan rushed over to express her worry and find out if all was well.

"Don't be silly," Sue said. "I just went out with some friends from work."

Timidly, Susan raised the other topic on her mind. "Did you scream last night?"

"No," Sue said, her brow furrowed in confusion.

"Did you have a bad dream?"

"No." Sue eyed her young neighbor as if her trolley had slipped off the track.

"Well, last night I heard a scream. It sounded like someone was murdered over here."

Sue just rolled her eyes and sent Susan home.

In the summer of 2001, one of the Schooling cats had a litter of kittens. William—and every kid in the neighborhood—came by to see the little balls of newborn fur. William wanted a kitten and brought his dad over to look at them. Rick told him he could have the white kitten with the double stripe down its back. Rick asked Susan, "When can we take the kitten home?"

"The kittens are already taken," Susan said.

As usual when someone said something Rick did not want to hear, he stood and stared as if willing the other person to change the response. Three nights in a row, he repeated his question. Each night, Susan told him that all the kittens were promised to other homes, and he responded in the same way.

Charlene was exasperated with Rick's refusal to understand Susan's response. "Just what part of 'No' don't you understand, Rick?"

Rick ranted about how they had disappointed William, then said, "Well, then you're just going to have to be the one the tells William to his face." Rick stomped out of the Schooling house, got William and returned. He thrust William in front of Susan and told her to tell him.

"William, my sister Betsy is taking that kitten with her to New York when she goes back to school."

All that week, William believed it when his dad told him again and again that they would be bringing that kitten home soon. Hurt blanched his young face and drove him to tears.

"See what you made William do?" Rick said.

Susan was too near tears herself to respond. Charlene stepped in and said, "I'm sorry, William, but your dad has known all along that you can't have that cat. It was promised to someone else."

Although he did not get one of the Schooling kittens, William soon did have a cat of his own. He called her Ana— naming her after the doomed tsarina Anastasia. Anastasia meant "able to live again."

Rick visited with a neurologist for an evaluation on September 12. He reported that he discontinued his use of Prozac and Adderol months ago. He complained of tingling in his extremities and chest, but no dizziness. He feared some loss of hearing, but said his taste and smell were good, except when he had sinus trouble.

The doctor concluded that Rick had no structural or pathological problems with his neurology, but he did have an anxiety disorder that made him tense, rigid, oversensitive, suspicious and stubborn. He recommended that Rick develop a detailed daily schedule with an hourly grid. He should post it in a conspicuous place and check it every hour. He suggested that Rick wear a wrist watch alarm to remind him to do so.

In the fall, William attended Melissa St. John's art class. One afternoon, all the other kids had been picked up from class and William volunteered to clean up spilled paint from the tables and floors while he waited for his ride. Rick arrived about a half hour late and exploded in anger— shrieking at William for getting a spot of paint on his shirt. Melissa took William aside to make sure he was all right. That was the last art class William attended that session.

Melissa suspected that CPS was not following through on her report. She called their offices to find out what they had done. The answer she got was disappointing. CPS called Sue McFarland. When she told them it was an accidental injury, Melissa's report was filed away.

Melissa was incredulous that CPS took the word of the wife of an accused abuser and did not interview William. She asked the CPS worker that if she had any concerns about a child's safety in the future, should she call the police instead?

The woman at the agency admitted that it would be better.

Everyone in CPS knew about the perilous situation at the agency. But it would be three more years before the state stepped in to assist with the case overload and backlog at the Bexar County office.

Melissa was not the only one getting reports of abuse from William. He told neighbor Carrie Miller that his dad had hit him with a baseball bat and the bat had broken. But William, who was wearing Speedos at the time, could not—or would not—point out any bruises on his body. Carrie did not put much credence in his story then, but later, it would come back to haunt her.

Next door to the McFarlands, Charlene often listened to Rick's loud and mean-spirited voice yelling at the boys when Sue was not home. And she heard the children crying in response. Many times, she thought about speaking to Susan about the yelling, but was concerned about overstepping her bounds.

One cold, rainy morning earlier that year, she saw William leave the house to catch the bus to school. As he walked out of the house, he screamed, "I hate you!"

Rick's head popped out the door and he bellowed, "I hate you, too!" Rick then slammed the door shut and locked it.

William tried to get back in to retrieve a school book he had forgotten. But no matter how much he pleaded, Rick would not unlatch the door and let him in.

13

In the fall of 2001, Sue's mother fell and broke her hip—she would never be the same again. For three months, Sue shared with other family members in the responsibility of caring for her mother. Every other weekend, she flew up to St. Louis. Sometimes Timmy tagged along and visited with his grandparents while Sue sat by her mother's bedside.

Ann told Sue she'd been advised to put a candy dish on the far side of the room to ensure that the nursing staff would have to pass by Mary Elizabeth on their way to the goodies. But Ann had not found the time to pick one up. Sue took on that responsibility and, of course, purchased the most colorful candy dish she could find.

The whole family was very concerned about their mother's ability to handle surgery to repair her hip. The situation turned critical before they reached a decision.

Ann was out of town on business at that time. Sue called to let her know the procedure was complete, "You're not going to believe this, but I think Mom is hallucinating. She woke up from surgery talking about window washers who were strippers."

Sue wanted to have neurological and psychological tests run on her mother. Ann was not sure if they should put her through that ordeal. Then Ann remembered something that made the testing unnecessary. The last time Mary Elizabeth had people in her home to wash the windows, the cleaners she hired also moonlighted as Chippendale dancers. To Mary Elizabeth, the difference between that suggestive dancing and stripping was irrelevant.

Upon that revelation, Sue said, "How am I going to go back to the hospital and explain that one?"

Mary Elizabeth Mitchell Smith passed away on January 9, 2002, at the age of 82. Because she was an active life-long volunteer in her community and church, the family requested that donations in her name be made to Northwest City Meals on Wheels and to the memorial fund at Webster Groves Presbyterian Church.

Sue's high school friend Sandy survived her breast cancer and adjusted to the new demands in her life in time to be there for Sue when she suffered the staggering loss of her mother. Sandy offered to stand by Sue's side for the funeral in St. Louis. But Sue insisted that there would be plenty of family there for her then. The time when she would really need Sandy was when she returned home.

Sandy, with her 4-year-old daughter, Leslie, traveled to San Antonio for a long weekend. Sandy felt the uneasy strain of a stressful marriage as soon as she crossed the threshold of 351 Arcadia.

It was obvious that the magical newlywed love that used to fill Sue and Rick's home had vanished as if it had never been. In response to Sandy's questions about the state of their relationship, Sue said, "Well, I just figured raising kids is a partnership." She added that she had resigned herself to sticking to it until the boys were grown.

That issue addressed, Sandy and Sue plunged into a couple of giddy days filled with laughter. Sue, Sandy, Leslie, Timmy, William and James all piled onto the trampoline, jumping and giggling. As if on cue, the three boys plopped down and sat cross-legged on the taut surface. With an impish twinkle in her eye, Sue looked at her kids and launched herself into the air. The boys flew up in her wake, struggling to keep their legs crossed as they dropped back down. Then, stomp, stomp, stomp—Sue kept going to keep them bouncing. The air filled with squeals of "Do it again! Do it again!"

During the visit, Sandy helped Sue with her plans for a big combined birthday party for William and Timmy the next weekend. They made a trip to a piñata store—a real novelty for Sandy and her daughter. For the birthday party, Timmy picked out a Harry Potter piñata that was taller than he was.

Sue prattled on with boundless excitement about the 25-foot-tall inflatable slide she rented for the occasion. Sandy thought she was even more excited about this party than the two boys, who were both about to explode from anticipation.

Rick accommodated their need to spend one-on-one time together by watching all four children whenever asked. One of these times, Sandy and Sue went to an art glass store—Sue was an avid collector.

Sandy eyed a pair of glass chili pepper earrings that she thought would make a fun memento of her trip. Then she got side-tracked and forgot all about them. A week later, a small box arrived in the mail. Sure enough, it was the earrings she loved—an unexpected gift from Sue.

On March 6, Sue sent an email to her sister, Ann. She pasted information about an American Airlines special and then wrote a note:

> *My in-laws are starting a war. They left when I came home last night, as they thought I would be at work all night. They told Rick that I don't make them feel welcome enough. Gee, it's such a delight having someone in your house that critiques all your moves*
>
> *They've told him I also don't spend enough time with my kids and that I have a drinking problem. I think the drinking thing started on Christmas day, after spending it in the hospital with Mom, I brought over a bottle of wine to their home and had two glasses. The true sign of an alcoholic not someone under a lot of stress. Then I had the nerve to criticize the treatment of patients at St. John's Hospital—or the lack thereof—in front of their daughter-in-law*

*Debbie who works there. In hind sight, I never should
have gone over there and let them make me play the
game of all the things I'm grateful for. That's when I
thought I really was going to lose it.*

*Now if I have one glass (mind you, not two) of wine
when I get home from work, they give me dirty looks
and tell Rick I've got a nasty drinking problem. They've
also decided the only reason I went to lunch with my
girl friends on Saturday was so I can drink. Even
though they've been in town for a week and I don't
have time to see my girlfriends any other time. Go figure, I didn't even have a drink as I was getting ready to
throw two consecutive birthday parties on Sunday. So
how can I make them feel welcome when I dread the
thought of them there each night when I get home . . .*

*Anyway, enough of my raving and ranting. We're
leaving on Saturday morning to go to LA for spring
break. This also means that my in-laws will be gone
when we get back!!! I ended up getting all of us air-
fare for $600 as I had two free tickets on Southwest.
We haven't told the kids so that it doesn't take their
focus off enjoying their grandparents. I got a great
deal on a couple of days at Disneyland and then we'll
sightsee Hollywood, etc. When they get up on Saturday morning we're telling them that they're going to
LA and they won't know about Disneyland until we
pull up to the property. They're going to flip. We'll be
home late the night of March 15th.*

The trip, however, almost didn't happen. The day before
they were to fly out, Rick asked Charlene if she would watch
the pets while they were in Disneyland. Charlene agreed
without hesitation.

Ten minutes later, a loud argument drifted through Charlene's open windows. Rick and Sue were on their front
porch. Sue said, "I want a divorce. I'm sick of getting my ass
up at five A.M. every day and you not doing anything. You
need to get a job."

"I have a job," Rick protested.

"You need to get a real job, Rick. A real job with a real paycheck. With real benefits and a real office. I'm done. I've had it."

"What about the kids?"

"The kids will live with me," Sue said.

"Maybe we should see a lawyer about that."

"Rick, *we* don't go see a lawyer. It doesn't work that way. You have your lawyers and I have my lawyers. They'll work it out."

Charlene leashed up her dogs and took them for a walk, leaving the house in the direction opposite from the McFarland house. When she rounded the corner, Rick and Sue were still out on the front porch. "Hi, Susan," she said.

"Rick thinks we are going to Disneyland tomorrow, but I've got news for him—we're not going."

"Well, whatever you decide, just let me know if you want me to take care of the dog."

"No. We are not going," Sue asserted.

A while later, Charlene went out to her guest house to wash some laundry. Rick came over and said, "Charlene, can you still look after Sally?"

"Sure," Charlene said. The silence that followed made her squirm. She looked at Rick and noticed that the goatee he had been sporting for the last few months was now gone. "Oh, you shaved your beard. I was just getting used to it."

"There is a certain someone over there that doesn't like it," he said.

The relationship between Sue and Rick perplexed Charlene. Sue was the breadwinner. She kept the home organized. And yet, she always consulted with Rick in the decision-making. Why? Rick did what he wanted, when he wanted. Still, she deferred to his wishes—even on the most minor things. Like the time Sue wanted to plant climbing jasmine on the side fence. She didn't do it because Rick overruled her—he objected to having to maneuver the mower around the irregular shape it would create.

Other friends understood Sue's behavior. They knew she

would always consult with Rick. Sue had a desperate desire
to believe her marriage—and her husband—were normal.

In April, Rick McFarland got busy fixing a household
problem. Back in January, the family dog Sally had wandered
off the property and into the street. Her leg was broken when
she was hit by a car. Rick now installed an underground elec-
tric fence to keep her contained in the yard.

He dressed for the occasion in a plaid shirt, jeans and a
miner's cap. He completed his ensemble with the perfect
accessory—a circular saw. For some reason, this tool was
Rick's implement of choice for digging the trenches in the
ground around his yard. Charlene took one look at her
neighbor and knew it was an amusing photo op. She grabbed
her camera and went next door.

She tried to get Sue to come out and pose with Rick. Her
coaxing irritated Sue. "I do not want to be in any picture
with him."

Unbeknownst to Charlene, Rick's exuberance for his
project had already run amok. He had cut down one of Sue's
four prized rosebushes in the process. It was more than a minor irritation to Sue—it was another in a long list of wrongs.
She clung to her anger as stubbornly as a grape juice stain on
carpet.

Her fury prompted Rick to write a conciliatory email:

*Dearest Susan, I know I deserve to be in the dog
house. I am really sorry about chopping the rose
bush. I promise to be more open and ask before doing.
Sincerely with much love. Rick.*

The email may have solved the immediate crisis, but it
was no magic elixir for the ills in the McFarland household.
By May, Sue was writing in her journal again.

*On Friday, May 17, I drove to Timmy's school after
work. As soon as I arrived, he threw up on me. The
teachers told me he had been lethargic all day. I told
Rick but he did not offer any explanation.*

On Monday, Timmy said he was not feeling well and Rick picked him up from school around 3. The teachers told Rick that he had not eaten and Timmy complained that his stomach hurt.

Two days later, preschool called and asked that Timmy be picked up because he was being abusive to the teachers. Later, I asked Rick what happened at school that day.

"It was partially my fault," he said. "I forgot to give Timmy his meds."

"What are you talking about?" I asked. "Timmy has been off meds for two months."

"I gave him 5 mg of Adderol on Friday and again on Monday but haven't given him any since."

I told Rick how distressed I was that he gave Timmy meds without asking me.

"I had every right to. I asked you about it at work a few weeks ago and you said you didn't want to discuss it at that time. Since you didn't bring the subject back up, I had every right to do what I wanted," he said. Then, he added, "I'm going to get a strap and spank Timmy."

"No. It's just as much your fault as it is Timmy's. You put him on meds twice in the last week and then you took him back off. The ups and downs could have caused Timmy's abusive behavior."

"Okay. I'll give him a lesser punishment, then."

After that entry, there was nothing more for two months. She did, however, take another step in her contemplation of divorce. She called George Dowlen, Dee Ann's husband and an attorney, to ask questions about community property laws in Texas. He assured her that any inheritance she received from her mother would be her sole property and would not have to be divided up in case of divorce.

While Sue pondered taking a dramatic step in her life, she did not break her stride. She even took on additional responsibilities. From May 28 through June 25, she reported for duty at the 379th Grand Jury. One of the indictments this body handed down was served on Richard Clemmer, who was accused of ripping off older people by building trust through religion and taking advantage of their loneliness. He was convicted in November and given 2 years probation.

Sue knew Clemmer. He owned a Texaco station near her home. She warned her friends that he was not trustworthy. Nonetheless, her husband did not avoid him. Soon, Rick would entangle Clemmer in a fatal web.

14

In the spring of 2002, Rick participated with a group of men in the Walk to Emmaus, a weekend retreat adapted, in the seventies, by the Methodist Church from an older Catholic program. This three-day spiritual renewal program was designed to develop servant-leaders who would then strengthen their local church.

As part of the experience, participants are supposed to bring along letters from others extolling their virtues. Rick asked Sue to write a letter praising his role as a father. She refused. Rick was stunned and wounded.

Some said that Rick was very sincere in these acts of spiritual immersion and transformation. Others believed he was just polishing his image to enhance the possibility that he would get custody of his sons if Sue carried through on her threats of divorce.

Sue and Julie Speer had met at a school that both their children attended, and had known each other for about two years. The two women had a chance encounter at the Houston Hobby Airport in June 2002. Julie thought Sue looked very stressed.

Sue talked to Julie about wanting to redo her master bedroom and then complained about the bathroom. "Rick got upset about the colors. He wanted to use gray. But I am the only one that uses the master bedroom."

That was the first indication Julie had that things were not going well in the McFarland household.

In June, Sue and Rick traveled to Cozumel with Bill and Molly Matthews. Over the long weekend, the couple snorkeled, relaxed and dined together nightly. Instead of being a renewing getaway, the trip was a precursor to the disintegration of Rick and Sue's relationship. Sue turned to her journal once again.

> Rick and the boys went up to St. Louis to have an extended visit with his family on July 13. I talked to Rick on July 24 and he told me that Timmy had behaved so badly in Bible school that his brother David had called him and asked that Timmy be put back on meds. When he left home, Timmy was on meds. Now Rick was telling me that he stopped the pills as soon as he got to his mother's house.
> "Why?" I asked him.
> "Because Mom insisted."
> "I'm ready to file for divorce," I told him and hung up the phone.
> I went upstairs to work on cleaning out Rick's office while he was gone. It was impossible to walk in the room because of all the boxes and trash strewn across the floor. He had resumed his compulsive shopping habits and there were unopened items everywhere. And he didn't just buy new stuff—he'd also bought polo type shirts at the Boysville thrift shop. They all looked too worn-out to wear but he did not seem able to stop himself from buying more.
> Rick started driving back with the boys on August 1. He stopped at his alma mater, Southwest Missouri State University in Springfield, Missouri, and took a nap in the Student Union. He allowed the boys to run wild and unsupervised on campus while he slept.
> On August 2, Rick called to tell me that he and the boys had just returned from an all-night stay at the

hospital in Pauls Valley, Oklahoma. "I drove until late and then we checked into a hotel," he said. "I decided to take a shower but didn't notice that the non-skid decals had come off the tub. I slipped and hit my hip."

An ambulance took Rick and the boys to the hospital where x-rays revealed that nothing was broken. Rick was prescribed pain medication and muscle relaxers for his discomfort.

"I'm going to take a nap since I didn't get any sleep last night," he told me. "Then I'll drive back to San Antonio."

Because the medications he was taking were a safety concern, I objected. "I'll catch a plane and drive you all home."

"I am capable of driving," he insisted.

The argument raged back and forth but finally Rick relented and agreed to wait until I got there to drive them home. I flew up to Dallas where I planned to rent a car and drive up to Pauls Valley. Then, I thought, I would drive the boys in the rental car and Rick could follow me back to the airport to return the rental.

But when I landed in Dallas, I had a voice mail message on my cell phone from Rick. "I'm feeling good. I'm driving to Dallas to pick you up."

On the drive home, all he could focus on was his desire to sue the hotel for negligence. Apparently, he had spent that morning calling several of his Christian Bible Study attorney buddies trying to establish grounds for a law suit.

"It was your fault you fell in the tub because you were groggy. Common sense is all the defense the hotel owner needs. Besides, Rick, even if you won, what would you end up with? A hotel in the middle of nowhere that carried a large note?" I argued. I believe I talked him out of the law suit. But who knows?

The last time Sue's close Amarillo friend Dee Ann saw Sue and Rick was in August 2002. Dee Ann did not think Rick was coping well—his conversations no longer made any sense and, for some odd reason, he'd shaved his head. When Dee Ann made a comment about Rick's bald pate, she expected Sue's usual response of joking that she had four boys instead of three, when Dee Ann pointed out something unusual about Rick. Instead Sue's tone turned derisive. "It's his new look," she said.

Picking up on Sue's attitude, Dee Ann mentioned that she had not heard Sue talk about the possibility of divorce since her mother was ill. She asked Sue what was happening.

"There is too much going on for me to try to file for a divorce right now," Sue told her.

Despite what Sue told her friend, circumstances arranged themselves in a manner that would make divorce more possible than ever before. Her inheritance from her mother gave her the money she needed to pay for one. And she no longer needed to face her mother's disapproval if she did go through with it. All she needed now was the gumption to take action.

Dee Ann and George were concerned about their friend because her self-confidence seemed to be at an all-time low. Sue had always been in control of herself and her family. Now she appeared to be at a crisis point and not as sure of herself as she was before.

In September, Sue drove up to St. Louis with a friend from work in a small rental truck. At her mother's house she met Pete, who drove up in his pickup from Kansas City. To Pete, loading up his truck and Sue's rental van was a chore, but he noticed that, for Sue, it was a grand adventure filled with excitement.

After the work was done, Pete didn't dawdle—he wanted to get back home before dark. As he drove off, he thought about how much he admired his younger sister. He knew how difficult it was to raise three children and maintain a professional career at the same time. But Sue did it and always with such a positive attitude. No matter what she did, Sue had fun doing it—and made sure that everyone around her was having a good time, too.

Later that month, Sue hosted a Southern Living party at her house for Julie Speer. A few days later, Rick and Sue went over to Julie's house to select the place settings they wanted to buy. Sue pointed to a green bowl she liked.

A strange look crossed Rick's face. "You never liked green before," he said. "What else has changed since we got married?"

15

More had changed than Rick had yet imagined. In early October, Sue called Julie and told her that she inherited some home furnishings and would like Julie's help in organizing and decorating the house. Julie asked about Rick's involvement, since he seemed to resent any decisions made without his input.

"Rick will not overrule decisions this time," Sue said. She went on to explain that she wanted shelves built by the fireplace to display special treasures. Julie made arrangements with a carpenter to do the work.

It was around this time that Rick began to exhibit an unusual interest in the sleeping arrangements in the Schooling household. "Which is your bedroom window, Charlene?" "Where does Susan sleep? In the guest house? Or in the main house?"

When Rick got only vague responses from Charlene, he asked Susan the same questions. For days, he questioned them about their domestic set-up every time an opportunity arose.

Charlene and Susan were both uneasy with the interrogation, but neither one of them could figure out what was going on in the convoluted thought processes of their neighbor. Later, they were certain of his motivation. They believed that Rick wanted to know exactly where each person would be so he could stage the murder of his wife without being observed.

• • •

Sue chronicled her life in her journal again.

> *A group of boys in the neighborhood were getting*
> *kicks out of playing ring and run—ringing the door-*
> *bell then running and hiding. It had gotten past the*
> *funny point. Rick's grand plan was to load the boys in*
> *the car with water guns, chase the kids down and*
> *shoot water at them. I threw a fit. Rick relented and*
> *just ran after them and told them to quit.*
>
> *One afternoon, the ringing and running started*
> *again. Rick hid behind the door waiting for their re-*
> *turn. When they did, he pelted the kid with his shoe.*
> *When I got home, he bragged about it. I was upset. I*
> *knew the kid could have gone home and made up a*
> *story telling his mother that he was attacked by Rick*
> *without provocation.*
>
> *"You are ridiculous," Rick said. "Call the mom*
> *yourself if it is such a big deal. With all the SBC*
> *[Southwestern Bell Corporation] smoothing over lan-*
> *guage you use, I'm sure you can handle the problem."*
>
> *"If I call, Rick, it will just look like I am cleaning*
> *up your mess."*
>
> *He made the call but to the wrong parent. Appar-*
> *ently, he did not know which kid he hit with his shoe.*

Later that month, Sue contacted Charles Parker, a private investigator. She complained that someone was sending
emails to her husband accusing her of committing adultery.
Whoever sent them, she told him, named hotels and restaurants she had visited on business trips. She suspected that
the sender might be someone from her church. Sue denied
the infidelity allegation and said that her husband believed
her. She wanted to know who was sending the emails.

Parker said he would try to set up a meeting with that person. The emails came from several addresses, but all of them
led back to ctsmith@mail.com. On October 17, Parker

emailed that address, telling the recipient, "I am looking for you. Will you contact me?"

Parker received no reply from the email, but he knew it must have arrived because it did not bounce back. He assumed the emails had stopped, since he never heard from Susan McFarland again.

16

One evening, Rick rushed over to the Schoolings' with an urgent request. As usual, he knocked on the far side window to get their attention. He was too intimidated by the dogs to make a direct approach to the front door whether the dogs were in or out.

Rick pleaded with the two women to come over to the house for a dinner party. He expressed distress because he did not know the guests and because some of them were Hispanic. "Could you and Susan come over and help us keep the conversation going?"

On the assumption that Sue had sent Rick over to offer this invitation, the two Schooling women cleaned up, dressed up and headed next door in record time. In fifteen minutes, they knocked on the front door. Through the sidelight, they saw that everyone was already seated for dinner.

Rick opened the door and said, "Yeah?"

"Well, we're here now, Rick," Charlene said.

"We're having dinner right now."

Turned around from her seat at the table, Sue looked toward the door, a puzzled frown on her face. Charlene realized Sue was clueless. To Rick, she said, "I thought you wanted us to come over."

"Oh, I thought I told you we didn't need you," Rick said.

Charlene and Susan returned home confused—as usual—by Rick's inexplicable behavior.

* * *

Sue amassed new friends in San Antonio quicker than a stray dog gathered fleas. Because of this expanded social network, the McFarlands and the Cromacks were not as close as they had been in St. Louis. Nonetheless, the Cromacks knew Rick and Sue's relationship was worsening before Sue told Margot that she "did not know the person she was living with anymore."

They thought that Rick was decompensating all over the board since the move to Texas. The change was so subtle and gradual that they did not notice it at first. When they did, the intense drama of the transformation he underwent over the past two years hit them like a thunderclap on a quiet summer night.

His speech pattern had changed—his speaking becoming so halting that it was difficult to follow a sentence to its end. He demonstrated a deterioration in his judgment. And he seemed oblivious to it all.

They urged him to get medical help—they hoped the problem was physical and easily resolved. Doug and Margot were medical professionals, but their experience was in intensive care units and emergency rooms. They felt lost in the face of Rick's degrading mental health. They tried to interact with him to uncover the underlying problem, but since they'd known him, Rick always had a knack for pulling others out without offering any forthright revelations about his own thoughts or feelings.

In October, the McFarlands drove up to San Marcos to join Pete Smith's former wife Debbie and her family for a Southwest Texas State University football game. Afterwards, they all went to a frat house for a pizza feast. Sue and Debbie made plans to spend Thanksgiving together in San Antonio for the third year in a row.

Blanca Hernandez and Sue McFarland had been friends for four years. They called each other almost every day at work and sometimes met for lunch. To be honest, though, Sue would rather shop than eat. Many lunch hours, she hopped from shop to shop and returned to work laden with bags and packages.

She was even known to combine the two with impeccable timing. Friends recalled occasions when she sat down to lunch, ordered her meal, made a quick dash to a shop, returned with her purchase and sat back down at the table just as her order was served.

On Saturday, November 2, Blanca went to the Target store near Route 281 and Jones Maltsberger Road. She knew Sue was working in her office at Southwestern Bell that day.

As she entered the store, she saw Timmy exiting the door. She scooped him up in her arms and asked, "Who are you here with, Timmy?"

"I'm with my dad."

"Where is your dad?"

"I don't know."

Blanca took Timmy inside, but did not spot Rick right away. She got a man in the store to check out the men's room. Then she saw Rick in line at the checkout. She walked over to him and said, "Rick, Timmy was all by himself and trying to go outside."

Rick shrugged it off and changed the subject to that night's dinner plans.

After Sue finished up at work, she ran some errands and returned home at 3 P.M. When she arrived, Rick left, promising he would be back with the hardware for his project with the armoire and would have it all finished by the time the baby-sitter arrived at 5:30.

He did not get back, however, until 6:30. Rick and Sue then went to Josephine Street for dinner at the Liberty Bar with Blanca and Gil Hernandez and Molly and Bill Matthews. Rick never said a word to Sue about the odd occurrences that day. He did, however, speak to Gil and Bill about his run-in with the manager at Eckerd after he returned Halloween costumes to the store.

The next morning, Sue left the house at 7 to take William to Houston for a Tomatis session. Tomatis is a behavior modification program designed to help children and adults by teaching sensory integration—the ability to tune out distractions and develop listening skills. Rick stayed home and watched James and Timmy. As Susan related in her journal:

> *I called Rick from Houston and asked what they had done and if he had picked up milk.*
>
> *"You don't need to constantly check up on me," he snapped. "We decided not to go to church so you'll have to pick up milk on your way home."*
>
> *When William and I were nearing the house, William said, "Dad isn't ever allowed in the store again where he was returning things yesterday. The manager told him to get out and never come back or he is calling the police."*
>
> *"Where is this store, William?" I asked him.*
>
> *"Next to Baskin Robbins. Me and James and Timmy think the manager should have let him take the stuff back."*
>
> *When I finally got home in the pouring rain at 9:30 that night, the house was a mess. Rick and the kids had done nothing but watch TV and go shopping at Target.*
>
> *On Monday, my friend Blanca called. "Do you know why Rick got thrown out of Eckerd's?"*
>
> *"Where did you hear that?" I asked her.*
>
> *"Saturday night at dinner, Rick told Gil and Bill about it. He asked them if the manager had the right to prohibit him from ever entering the store again.*
>
> *I was blown away that he would actually discuss being such a jerk with our friends. But that was not all Blanca had to tell me about the weekend. On Saturday, she said, she caught Timmy running out of Target and was afraid he'd get hit by a car. She took him into the store to Rick who acted like it was no big deal.*
>
> *Rick and I have talked and talked about this—he knew he wasn't supposed to let the kids roam around*

stores without supervision. One time, he let little
Timmy go to the bathroom all by himself. And he lost
him in Wal-Mart. Wal Mart closed down the whole
store to find Timmy. That didn't seem to make any impact on Rick.

Blanca said she thinks Rick is mentally ill. She
said he has such poor judgment that I should not let
him take care of the kids.

That night, I asked Rick, "What happened at
Eckerd?"

Instead of answering the question, Rick expressed
his shock that our friends would tell me about that. I
didn't dare let him know that William was the one
who let the cat out of the bag.

"It's humiliating for me when you get thrown out
of where I shop on a regular basis," I told him.

Did he apologize? No. He got annoyed with me for
thinking it was a big deal.

"And," I continued. "It is totally inappropriate for
the kids to be a party to you badgering the manager. I
don't want you to take the kids with you to the store
anymore."

I am afraid for the kids' safety. Rick does not insist
that they stay with him when he is shopping. I'm
scared someone will harm or kidnap one of my boys.

William was scheduled for another class in Houston
on Saturday, November 9, at 9 A.M. I planned on taking him myself. But on Thursday, Rick called me at
work again and again insisting that he take William. I
told him that I thought his sleeping habits made it unsafe for him to get up at 5:30 in the morning and
drive to Houston.

He called back later and offered a compromise—
he would drive down on Friday after school and
spend the night with a good high school friend. That
sounded reasonable so I told him he could take
William.

"I'll leave as soon as school is out," he said.
"What are you going to do with our five- and
nine-year-olds?"
"I'm sure we could figure something out," he said.
We? Right. That meant me. I made arrangements
with my friend Molly to look after them until I got off
of work.

On Friday, November 8, over her lunch hour, Sue made her
first visit to her new divorce attorney, Christine Tharp. "My
husband is mentally unstable and irrational. He overreacts to
some situations while not taking appropriate safety precau-
tions with our children."

She added that Rick was becoming more secretive and
was prone to freaking out and going off on her. He was out
every night and neighbors reported that he was driving aim-
lessly up and down their streets.

Tharp came to the conclusion that it would turn into a
real battle once Rick found out about the divorce. Fights
about separate property, community property and the custody of the children loomed on the horizon. Tharp encouraged Sue to feel free to leave if she needed some time away.

As she left the attorney's office, Sue called her supervisor
Gary Long and apologized that she was running late. It was
unusual for Sue not to be on time unless she made arrangements to alter her schedule beforehand. After arriving back
in the office, she explained to Gary that she had been seeing
an attorney about a divorce. The papers, she said, would be
served in a couple of weeks, but she did not want Rick to
know about her plans until then. Gary noticed Sue's emotional distress, but did not press her for her reasons.

For the next couple of weeks, Sue and her attorney had
frequent phone calls and meetings. Sue's anxiety was building day by day as Rick's behavior became more and more irrational. "Life with him was so unbearable, I asked him to
leave," she told her attorney.

On the same day of her first visit, Sue's arrangements for

the care of the two younger boys required Rick to drop them off at 4 P.M. Molly planned to take them with her to her daughter's soccer game. At 4:45—still no Rick—Molly had to leave for the game. She called her cousin, who came to the house to wait for Rick.

In addition to planning for the care of the boys, Sue also orchestrated a special treat for William after his class in Houston. Friends at the Witte Museum in San Antonio set it up for William and Rick to join a private tour group to view the *Titanic* exhibit.

At 9 P.M. on Saturday, November 9, I was concerned that Rick and William were not home from Houston. I called and asked how close they were to San Antonio.

"I haven't left Houston yet," Rick told me. "I got caught up shopping at Ikea."

"Don't spend any more money, Rick. Our house is overflowing with stuff now."

He said he wouldn't buy anything—he was just shopping—so I moved on to my bigger concern. "I don't think it is safe for you to be driving back so late."

"No big deal," he said. "I slept five hours this afternoon and feel well-rested."

"You didn't take William to the Titanic *exhibit?"*

"William had fun with his friends so he really didn't miss anything."

I expressed my disappointment at his irresponsibility and my embarrassment that my friends had gone out of their way to make special arrangements and he just didn't bother to go.

"You're making a big deal out of nothing," he told me.

Again, I pleaded with him to stay over in Houston and drive back in the morning. This time, he agreed. I awoke at 2 A.M., Rick was asleep in my bed. I went outside and looked in the car. It was full of shopping bags from Ikea.

On Tuesday morning before I left for work, I volunteered to pick up William from swimming at 5:30. Rick was pleased and said he would count on it.

I left work at 5:15 so that William would not have to wait. As I approached the high school, I saw Rick driving south on Broadway. I called his cell. "Did you just pick up William?" I asked.

"No. I didn't need to—William and James are at home—they came home on the school bus."

"You left them home alone?"

"Why are you so upset? They are 9 and 11 now and I have Timmy with me."

"Why did you have to leave them by themselves?"

"I had to run errands."

"Rick, how would you feel if you needlessly left work to pick up one of the kids?"

"You're making a big deal over nothing."

I stopped by the grocery store to pick up lunch snacks for school the next day and to get a loaf of French bread for our spaghetti dinner. Rick called. "James is hungry. Pick up some Wendy's on the way home."

"We're having spaghetti, tonight," I told him.

He ridiculed me for not wanting to pick up fast food. He didn't seem to see any difference in feeding the kids spaghetti or a burger from Wendy's.

That Wednesday, on the way back to work after helping out with Junior Achievement, Sue called Dee Ann in Amarillo. "I'm getting a divorce. I just can't take it anymore. He won't pull his load. He lets the kids wander off. I've asked him to get a job and he won't," she confided. "But don't say anything to anyone, because I am keeping it a secret from Rick."

Dee Ann promised she would not mention it. Sue added that Rick was acting too crazy. "He gets in my face and screams at me. I don't have time to fight with him anymore."

The other concern Sue shared with Dee Ann was financial. Her sister Ann wanted to distribute $15,000 each to Sue and her two brothers as part of their inheritance. Sue didn't want Rick to know about the money now that the divorce was in progress.

After talking to Dee Ann, Sue called George Dowlen to find out if he was familiar with her attorney, Christine Tharp. She told George that Rick was irresponsible and unable to care for their three sons. When Sue got home that day, William and James were there, but no one else.

17

On Tuesday, November 12, Sue opened a new bank account in her name only at the River City Federal Credit Union. She used co-worker Jennifer Biry's address for any mail. Then she got a cash advance of $7,500 from a credit card to retain her attorney.

She summarized the next few days in her journal.

Rick came home and told me that he attended the Howard PTO at lunchtime and found out that it was unsafe for kids weighing under 80 pounds to ride without booster seats so he bought two for James and Timmy for his car. "You are abusing Timmy by letting him use only a seat belt in your car," he accused.

His words stung and upset me but he continued. "It is about time I found something that you are doing wrong," he said, a smug expression on his face. "I researched and found out that only 200 kids are kidnapped each year by strangers—a lot more are killed by riding without booster seats. So, you are guiltier of child abuse than I am when I let the kids run around the store unsupervised."

He then told me that he'd made an appointment for me with the Safety Council to have my booster seats inspected on Friday. When I objected that I had plans that day, Rick snapped, "You are neglecting your kids."

In the morning, I changed the appointment Rick set to one that day at lunch. I followed the expert's advice in selecting seats for Timmy and James.

Rick took the boys out to dinner that evening and I planned to catch up with them at the Woodridge family literacy night after they ate. While everyone was gone, I decided to search Rick's office to see if he had any credit cards he had concealed from me. But the door was fastened shut with a chain and a combination lock. I couldn't believe it—he'd locked me out. I don't know what he is hiding.

On Friday afternoon, I called and found Rick at Target. He said he was buying a five point booster seat for Timmy. "Why didn't you buy the one the Safety Council was selling at the school?"

"I needed to return the one I bought Wednesday."

"If you bought the $40 one from the Safety Council, you could still return the $60 one to Target."

"$20 is no big deal," Rick said. The seat I bought James is safer than the one you bought from the Safety Council.

I found that hard to believe. I am not convinced that he cannot tell the difference between the truth and a lie.

That day, two seemingly unrelated events occurred. Guy Chipman took his Suburban to the Wash Tub Car Wash to be detailed. Then he dropped off the vehicle along with one remote-equipped alarm key at the Texaco service station. For a small fee, Richard Clemmer would sell the vehicle for him and Chipman would not have to hassle with potential buyers. Chipman did not leave any personal items in the car.

Just a short drive away, Rick McFarland sat down at one of his computers and accessed Sue's computer. He downloaded files from her computer to his. The documents included Sue's journal, client and custody questionnaires that Sue filled out for her attorney and a list of property and assets. Rick was now aware of Sue's plans to file for divorce. He began to make plans of his own.

18

Sue talked to Ann about her inheritance from their mother. She wanted checks to be sent to Jennifer's address so that Rick could not get his hands on them.

"I'm no longer looking at that money for the kids' education. I'm looking at it as a cushion to build our future." She added that she knew she would have to support Rick for a while after the separation.

The conversation moved to talk about the boys. Ann pointed out that even if Sue did get sole custody, Rick would be entitled to regular visitation.

"I hope I will be able to convince the judge that Rick should only be allowed to have visitation with one boy at a time," Sue said.

Saturday, November 16, Blanca Hernandez was sitting in her living room in front of the window that faces the street. She saw Rick drive up the street slowly while staring at her house. Then he turned around and drove past her again. When he repeated this action seven times, Blanca called Sue to find out if she was okay and told her what Rick was doing.

At 9 P.M., Charlene heard a noise coming from Ned and Harriet Wells' house at 356 Arcadia across the street. The house was for sale and although one of them dropped by every day, they were no longer living there.

Peering out the window, she saw Rick McFarland dressed all in white. He was weed-eating around the curbs at the

Wellses' house. How odd, Charlene thought—Rick never trims his own yard without being nagged by Sue.

Rick was up and down throughout Saturday night so I was tired when I woke up Sunday morning. "What were you doing all night?" I asked him.

"I was working on the laundry," he said.

It didn't look like much laundry had been done so I asked him, "What else did you do?"

"I was getting caught up on business."

After church, I took the boys to lunch and the zoo. We got back at 3:30 and I asked Rick what he had been doing.

"Hooking up the GameCube to surround sound," he said.

Great. Our home computer is not working and here he is enhancing the audio on a game.

After November 17, Sue made no more entries in her journal. She did not chronicle the last eight days of her life.

19

That same day, after a trip to the zoo and the all-too-familiar confrontation with Rick upon returning home, Sue got a phone call from neighbor Carrie Miller. It was almost time for Wesley's birthday party that afternoon and she wondered if Sue would be bringing her boys over. "Did you get the invitation Wesley hand-delivered?" she asked.

"No," Sue sighed. "Rick probably didn't give it to me, as usual."

The five McFarlands made it to the party and Sue even brought a present for Wesley—a Ouija ball that talked to you when you threw it in the air. She spent time with Wesley showing him how to play with it.

At one point during the party, Carrie noticed that Rick was nowhere to be seen. Concerned that he might be roaming around in her house, Carrie asked Sue if she knew where he was.

"He said he went to Home Depot," Sue said, "but he's probably lying to me again."

After the party, Austin Hardeman, another neighborhood boy, went over to the McFarlands' with William to play on the trampoline. They were soon joined by Wesley. When the play became too aggressive, a distressed Austin ran off.

Sue looked down from her bedroom window and realized Austin was no longer there. She sent Wesley home, gathered up her boys and rushed over to the Hardeman house. "What happened to Austin? Is he here?" Susan asked.

"Yes he is here. He ran home crying. Where were you? You were supposed to be watching them," Austin's mother Karen said.

"I looked out the window and Austin was gone. I'm sorry, Karen."

Carrie and Wesley showed up at Karen's house. After a brief conference, the three mothers chastised the boys for their behavior. The kids made up and headed to the backyard to play.

"Did Rick get back?" Carrie asked.

"I don't know," Susan said.

"Where did he go?"

"I called and he said he went to the bank."

"What?!" Karen added, "Susan, the bank's not open."

"I don't know where he is or what he is doing. He always lies to me."

In unison, her friends said, "Well, yeah . . ."

"I've had it with that man. I need to go find where he is."

While Sue had lunch with Jennifer Biry the next day, Christine Tharp called her cell phone to discuss serving divorce and eviction papers on Rick. Sue wanted the papers served within the week. In addition to wanting it all over, the coming week was the least stressful in her monthly work routine. Tharp advised her to wait until the Monday after Thanksgiving—the holiday might interfere with the efficiency of working with the courts. However, the first week of every month was the worst time of all for Sue to be distracted from her job.

After the call, Sue poured out her worries to Jennifer. She said she was very nervous about the coming week. She'd been bringing the boys into bed with her to make sure there was no room for Rick. She hoped he'd believe that they came there on their own. But he figured out it was all at her instigation and got very upset.

Sue said that she'd made reservations for Rick to fly to St. Louis to spend time with his family over Thanksgiving—

they wouldn't be going up at Christmas, so she thought he'd like the idea. Sue told him she was going out to Amarillo for the holiday so he'd be more willing to go to St. Louis. She really planned to stay home, Sue confided to Jennifer, and make Thanksgiving dinner with all the trimmings for a couple of friends from Houston, but felt if she couldn't get Rick to visit his parents, she would have to go to Amarillo. She did not want to spend the long weekend with Rick.

Sue pulled out a yellow sheet of paper filled with hotel information. Sue told Jennifer, she'd made arrangements for a room for Rick at a nearby hotel—she pointed to the second one on her list—so he would have someplace to go after the papers were served.

Jennifer told Sue about her plans for Tuesday, November 26, and Sue offered to baby-sit for her. Unlike most of the commitments she made in her life, Sue did not keep that promise.

Later that day, Sue sent an email to her sister Ann:

> *Rick is getting more secretive and remote by the day. Maybe he's doing some of his own plotting and planning. In my dreams . . .*
>
> *My attorney, Christine Tharp, cannot get everything ready this week as she is going to be in court. Then next week is a short week due to Thanksgiving. The following week is out of the question for me work-wise. So this may have to go on another THREE weeks. UGHHHHHHH!*
>
> *Unbeknownst to Rick, I made him reservations to travel to STL over Thanksgiving. I'm going to talk him into going, as I don't think I could stand 4 days straight of him. The tension is killing me. He can tell his parents since we aren't coming to STL for Xmas he wanted to take some time to visit with them. Now I only have to convince him . . .*

. . .

At 356 Arcadia, Shiner, the Wellses' black Labrador, was still in residence in the backyard behind a sturdy gate with a complex lock. Harriet came by every day to feed him and planned to move him as soon as the fencing was erected at their new home.

At 10 P.M., Charlene and Susan noticed that Shiner was out of the yard and in the front of the house. They assumed that Harriet or Ned must be at the house. At midnight, they spotted Shiner padding his paws down the street.

Susan coaxed the wandering dog back into the yard and discovered the gate hanging wide open. She knew someone had to have been on the Wells property. It was impossible for Shiner to have unlatched the gate on his own.

Before 8 A.M. on Wednesday morning, Rick called Sue's work phone and left a message: "Susan, Rick. If you feel you need some time away this Thanksgiving, feel free to do so. I'm going to stay here in San Antonio. Do whatever you think you need to do."

But Sue was not at work, she was at home that morning with Julie Speer. Julie was helping her prep the house for the birthday party she was throwing for Margot Cromack that weekend. Margot's husband Doug called Susan a few weeks earlier because he wanted to throw a fiftieth birthday party for his wife. "Can you help me? I don't know who to invite," he said.

"First of all, Doug, you don't throw a birthday party at your house, because if you do, she'll have to clean up afterwards."

Sue and Julie worked to assimilate the pieces Sue hauled back from St. Louis in September into the existing interior design. Before they got down to the task at hand, Sue said that the plan to build shelves by the fireplace had to be put on hold for now. Around 11:30, they were near the front door deciding what to do with the stackable baskets when Rick drove by at a slow speed.

"Rick is bizarre," Sue said with apparent irritation.

A half hour later, the two women were in the living room near the window. Rick went down the road in his white van. Julie said, "He's driving by again."

Sue just lowered her head.

That afternoon, Rick McFarland and one of his sons pulled up to the Texaco station on Austin Highway, near his home. The owner, Richard Clemmer, noticed he was lecturing his son, but the boy did not appear to be paying any attention. Rick then looked toward the lot at a white Jeep and a blue-and-gray Suburban adorned with FOR SALE signs.

Rick got the key to the Jeep from Clemmer and took the car out for a test drive. He returned in twenty minutes and got the key for the Suburban. He didn't return with it for two hours.

When he got back, he said, "My wife likes the Suburban but I like the Jeep—I like its leather interior and it would fit in the garage better than the Suburban." Rick wrote a false name and telephone number in the phone message book and said he was going out of town for a few days and would get back to Clemmer later.

The next day Sue talked to Dee Ann about coming out to Amarillo with her boys to spend Thanksgiving with her.

"I'll get busy cooking," Dee Ann replied.

"I don't need anyone else making me feel guilty," Sue snapped.

"I'm not trying to make you feel guilty, Sue. I'm excited about cooking. We've got fifteen other people coming that day."

Sue's voice softened, "Could you get a baby-sitter for the Friday after Thanksgiving, so we could go out?"

As soon as she got off of the phone, Dee Ann arranged for the girl next door to take care of the kids that night.

Rick called the Texaco station and spoke to Fernando Adamez. "A friend of mine test-drove the white Jeep you have for sale. It broke down at a Diamond Shamrock on

Austin Highway. Will you tell the owner about the Jeep?"

Adamez looked across the street at the Diamond Shamrock there. A white Jeep was parked at the gas pumps. A while later, he noticed it hadn't moved, so he grabbed the keys off the board in the office and went over to it. The key fit the ignition, but the Jeep would not start. He pushed it out of the way of customers and went back across the street. Later, Clemmer got the Jeep back to the Texaco station.

On Friday, November 22, Rick stopped by to see Clemmer. He told him about his friend's problem with the Jeep and wanted to know if it could be fixed. He said that his wife liked the Suburban better. And again, he told Clemmer that he was going out of town, but would be back to see him on Monday or Tuesday.

That same night, the McFarland, Hernandez and Matthews families planned to get together for dinner. The original scenario called for the three families to rendezvous at Joe's Crab Shack. When Blanca objected to that restaurant, they selected EZ's for the meeting point.

Sue surprised everyone by showing up with her kids but without her husband. When asked where Rick was, Sue laughed. "I didn't tell Rick we weren't going to Joe's Crab Shack."

Over dinner she told Blanca that Rick had spent all the money in their bank account. "I gave him a deadline to return all of the money," she said.

Susan McFarland had three more days to live.

20

On the morning of Saturday, November 23, Blanca left a message on Sue's phone. When Sue returned the call, she asked if Blanca had seen Rick. Her husband, she said, had not returned until midnight the night before. When she asked him where he had been, he refused, at first, to answer. Later he told her he had been at the neighbors', but did not specify which ones.

About 9:30, dressed in gray sweats, Rick pulled his white minivan up to a gas pump at the Texaco service center. He asked Raymond Ross to pump $10 worth of gas. Then, he asked to look at the Suburban. Ross went to the office and grabbed the key off of the board.

While Ross pumped the gas and checked the air in the tires, Rick opened the driver's-side door and the hood. He walked back and forth between the two several times, then went to the office and grabbed the key to the restroom. In ten or fifteen minutes, Rick returned to the office, had a drink of water, fixed a cup of coffee and paid for his gas.

Ross asked, "Do you need anything else?"

"No," said Rick sitting down on a chair. "I'm just killing some time." He sat quietly, sipping on his coffee. Five minutes later, he left.

Ann called Sue on her cell phone and caught her in Sam's Club picking up food and supplies for Margot's party on

Sunday. Ann asked why she was throwing a party at a time when so much else was going on in her life.

"I feel sorry for Doug," she said. "It's his wife's fiftieth birthday and he doesn't know what to do. Besides," Sue added, "I don't want to be home alone with Rick, and the party keeps my mind off waiting for it all to be over."

Doug was running his own birthday-related errands that day, but he had a co-conspirator on hand to keep Margot off the scent of his plans. Her college buddy Tom—a frequent visitor to their home—had flown in to keep Margot looking the other way at all times. Margot knew Doug was up to something, but she couldn't quite figure out what.

On this weekend before Thanksgiving, plans were all in place for another boisterous Christmas celebration in San Antonio. This year as always, the multi-cultural spirit of this former mission town turned the urban center into a jubilant city of lights.

The Fiesta de Luminarias brightened the Riverwalk. Yards and yards of light strings hung from the 100-foot cypress trees that spread their branches across the water—180,000 colorful, twinkling lights in all. Thousands of luminarias—candles in sand-filled paper bags—lined the walkways as a symbol of the lighting of the way for the Holy Family.

Festive boats cruised the river filled with carolers, bell choirs and performers for the hearing-impaired—groups from churches, corporations, civic organizations and schools. The Riverwalk was also home to Las Posadas, a reenactment of the search for shelter by Mary and Joseph on the night of the birth of the Baby Jesus. Bearing candles, the actors were joined by a mob of spectators that followed them to the end of their journey.

San Antonio, like nearly every city, had a holiday parade, but it boasted of one big difference—San Antonio's procession floated on the river. It began when the mayor pulled the switch to illuminate the thousands of lights on the Riverwalk. The one-hour parade draws 150,000, who watch while dining at sidewalk restaurants or peering out the windows of offices towering over the river or sitting on the grass-covered rows at La Villita's outdoor Arneson River Theatre. Millions more watch the live television coverage from the comfort of their homes.

Near the Riverwalk, a forty-foot tree was erected at the Alamo and festooned with lights and enormous decorations. At the Market Square, people and pets arrive for the annual blessing of the animals. Near the Justice Center, the San Fernando Cathedral stood like a beacon with every architectural line detailed in white lights. The Riverwalk and its surroundings—always a special place—was transformed into a vision of magic for the holidays.

The first event that put all these plans in motion this year—as every year—was the Seventeenth Annual Light the Way at the University of the Incarnate Word. Sue took her boys to observe this long-standing tradition with Molly Matthews and Blanca Hernandez and their children. She told Molly that she had not invited Rick to come along.

The event began at 7:30 in the McDermott Convocation Center with guests of honor Archbishop Patrick Flores and Singer Patsy Torres. After carols were sung by a children's choral group, a candlelight procession wended its way through the campus grounds now aglow with endless strings of lights. Around the trunk of every tree, white lights twinkled round and round and up into far-reaching branches. Student volunteers strung the grounds with more than 850,000 lights. The whole campus glowed like the doorway to heaven.

In sharp contrast to the serene, sanctified celebration at the University of the Incarnate Word, the SBC Center up Interstate Highway 35, was rocking and raw. The Rolling Stones were in town and Rick McFarland was there.

From Keith Richards's opening riff on "Street Fighting Man" to the encore performance of "Jumpin' Jack Flash," Rick grooved in the raucous retro night. The high point for many in the audience that evening was "Satisfaction." Keith

Richards shared a mike with Deborah Harry of Blondie to wail out the frustrations of not being able to get any satisfaction, while behind them the famous Stones tongue logo was set on fire.

In just two days, Rick would take action to find his own personal satisfaction, heedless of the impact on others. And when he did, the flames would light the night again.

21

On Sunday, November 24, Sue took the boys to church. She was raised Presbyterian and wanted to establish the boys in the same denomination—instead of Rick's Methodist faith. It was important to her for the boys to have a strong church home now that the family was unraveling.

Blanca, Gil, Molly and Bill arrived at the McFarlands' house at 2 to help Sue get ready for Margot Cromack's birthday party that evening. Rick did not assist in the preparations, but instead stayed outside puttering around in the yard. Doug dropped in to check on the progress of the party preparations. To help out, he took the three McFarland boys to McDonald's. As he left, he spotted Rick in the backyard—the expression of rage on Rick's face shocked him.

When Margot approached 351 Arcadia Street at 4 o'clock that afternoon, all the pieces of the puzzle slid into place. An enormous hand-painted banner hung high on the columns of the front porch proclaiming wishes for a happy fiftieth birthday.

Inside, everything was perfection. The recently acquired antiques easily fit in with the new decor. The dining room walls wore a fresh coat of paint. Mary Elizabeth's silver gleamed on her daughter's table. Food was everywhere—cheese, crackers, fruit, brownies, Swedish meat balls and lots and lots of champagne.

The pièce de resistance was the birthday cake—a huge carrot cake covered with cream cheese frosting and decorated with miniature plastic symbols that were meaningful and significant to Margot.

Everyone who had kids brought them to the celebration. Doors opened and closed as the children raced from the trampoline, into the house for food or drink and back outside again.

Early in the party, Rick asked Molly Matthews where they had all gone over the weekend. Without answering him, Molly ran to Susan. "What should I tell him?"

"Tell him whatever he wants to know," Sue said. "I have nothing to hide."

After not getting a response from Molly, Rick turned to her husband, Bill, and expressed his distress that everyone was intentionally deceiving him.

Sue talked to Rick when she wanted him to fetch sodas or other refreshments during the party, but otherwise did not speak to him. For a while, Rick circulated, talking about the Rolling Stones concert. He told anyone who would listen that he bargained down the $300 asking price on his ticket to $50. Most did not believe him. They figured he had paid $300, but did not want Susan to know.

At some point, Rick drifted away, went upstairs and fell asleep. No one noticed his absence until a crisis arose. Gaga Sikes, a frail man in his eighties with a history of heart trouble, became ill and everyone worried it was a heart attack or a stroke. Although Margot and Doug had not worked together for years as a medical team, the nurse and doctor fell back into their old routine without a word. They cared for Gaga until the emergency medical technicians arrived to take over. About the same time the techs got on the scene, the phone rang.

The caller was Susan's dentist, Dr. Dirk DeKoch. He was responding to the message Sue had left earlier in the weekend about needing an appointment because her temporary crown had worked loose. They set up a visit for 8 A.M. the next morning.

After nearly everyone had gone home, Sue sat in the backyard with Margot and Doug and a few other stragglers. Margot glowed with pleasure over the great food, good people and ceaseless champagne that all came together to celebrate her fiftieth year. Sue was relaxed and contented reflecting on a job well done. Watching her guest of honor revel in the night, and seeing all who attended having a good time, gave Sue a wealth of enjoyment. More than anything, it had been such a relief to put her personal problems on hold for a few glorious hours of entertaining.

Fernando Adamez arrived for work at the Texaco service center on Austin Highway at 7 A.M. on Monday, November 25. When he left work the previous day, the two-toned Suburban for sale was sitting in front of the gas pumps near the road. Now it was gone.

On that same morning, Sue arrived on time for her appointment with the dentist carrying a cup of Starbucks coffee. Dr. DeKoch replaced her temporary crown with a permanent one and repaired a chip on a lower front tooth. She talked about the elderly man who had a heart attack at her party and how lucky he was that it happened there, since there were so many doctors in her house at the time. Susan left at 8:30 and headed to work.

Upon her arrival, she realized that someone had retrieved the messages from her phone. She knew it had to be Rick—he had set up the voicemail on her phone at work and on her cell phone. Sue called Blanca Hernandez.

"You need to change your passwords and greetings," Blanca advised.

"What do you think about me going to Amarillo for Thanksgiving?" Sue asked.

"I think you should stay in town. Rick might get upset if you try to leave with the boys. You can come over to my house so you don't have to be around Rick," Blanca offered.

After a short discussion, Sue conceded that Blanca was right and said she would not leave town.

Later, Sue talked to Dee Ann and shared Blanca's concerns. She expressed uncertainty about what Rick might do if she spent Thanksgiving with Dee Ann.

"Then bring Rick with you if you want—we'll keep him busy. Whatever you need to do is fine."

The next call came from Molly Matthews. Sue told her she was still thinking about going to Amarillo. "Rick is angry with me," she confided, "because I am not talking to him." Molly and Sue then discussed the possibility of getting tickets for the Riverwalk parade the day after Thanksgiving.

Around 11 that morning, Sue's old Amarillo friend Dyann Folkner called. "I am so excited that you are coming to Amarillo."

"I'm not coming now," Sue said.

"I haven't seen the boys since December of 1998," Dyann complained. "Why did you change your mind?"

"A friend of mine thinks Rick might become violent if I take the boys."

"Do *you* think Rick would get violent?" Dyann asked.

"Yes," Sue said. "Rick has been really weird lately." She went on to recount examples of his strange behavior during the party the day before. She also told Dyann that she was filing for divorce.

Dyann consoled her by bringing up a mutual friend who was in a similar situation, then warned, "She has really turned her girls against their father."

"I would never turn the boys against Rick," Sue vowed.

"Is he acting any different with the boys?"

"No. But I really can't talk now because I don't want people at work to hear me. Call Dee Ann—she knows more about what's going on."

"I'm still going to try to see you this year even if I have to surprise you on your birthday."

"Now that would be a really good time," Sue said.

"I love you, Sue. We will get through this," Dyann reassured her.

Ann called and asked Sue about the success of her party. Sue told her about the medical emergency and how disturbing it was to her that Rick never came downstairs—not even when the ambulance arrived.

When Ann asked about the trip to Amarillo, Sue said, "Rick would make a big scene."

"What do you mean? Are you afraid of him?"

"No, no, no. He'll just make a big scene with the boys."

Sue called her niece just a few minutes before Kirsten's 1 P.M. staff meeting.

"What's new?" Kirsten asked.

Sue laughed. "A whole lot." She told her niece about the divorce, her "real aggressive attorney" and the serving of the papers in one week. "I have finally done it," she said, "because my friends have been telling me how strange he is." She recited a litany of Rick's bizarre and irresponsible behavior during the last few months.

The conversation turned to Thanksgiving preparations. Sue said that plans were off for Debbie and her family to come up from Houston and spend the day at her house as they had done the past two years.

"Is it safe for you to be there?" Kirsten asked.

"Rick might hurt me, but he would never hurt the kids."

"What are you going to do, Sue?"

"I'll do something."

After that call, Sue fulfilled a volunteer commitment— she drove over to Woodridge Elementary School and delivered muffins for a hospitality committee function at the school the next day. Margot's out-of-state friend Tom, an architect, taught a special lesson about buildings in cities and towns to Sue's Junior Achievement class that day.

Between 4 and 4:15 that afternoon, Frank Salazar left the office. He saw Sue, his supervisor, still at her desk. "See you tomorrow."

"Okay," Sue said.

Christine Tharp returned from the courthouse just past 5 and called Sue McFarland at work. They ran down the plan of action. Tomorrow, Sue would come to Tharp's office to review, approve or modify the Divorce Petition, Restraining

Order and the Order Setting Hearing to enable Tharp to file
the documents in court on December 2. While there, Sue
would sign the affidavits her attorney prepared and get ready
for the temporary hearing scheduled for the morning of
December 6.

Sue left work just before 6 P.M. and stopped by the H-E-B
Central Market grocery store on her way home. The evening
flowed through dinner and homework much like every other
school night.

At the Cromack house, discord reigned. For as long as her
children could remember, whenever a member of their family or the McFarland family had a birthday, they had gone to
one another's homes for cake and ice cream. Their mom had
not invited Sue and her family over, and Monday was their
mother's actual birthday. Margot insisted that they were not
breaking tradition. They'd had cake and ice cream together
the day before at the party and besides, she told them, she
was very tired. Her children were not mollified.

That evening, Margot went to bed earlier than usual. In
days, she would regret not giving in to her children's demand.

In the McFarland house that night, Sue helped her boys get
ready for bed. There were the usual complaints about taking
baths, the everyday whines about staying up just a little
longer. The night was all set to the typical rhythm of a
household that included three boys.

In the master bathroom, Sue prepared to begin her nightly
ritual—washing the days' makeup off her face, brushing her
teeth—all the habits of a lifetime.

In the midst of all these dull everyday concerns, while the
children slept in their beds, a spark flew out into the night.
Its glow revealed the plan Richard McFarland harbored in
his heart for days. It ignited the violence of Rick's ultimate
solution to his problems.

Fueled by a fiery rage, Rick beat the mother of his children over the head with a blunt object. He splattered her
blood all over that room. Droplets hid in the crevices of a

small wicker wastebasket and blended with the label of a bottle of bath gel in the shower. Blood dropped straight down on the bathroom scale and spattered the closet door. He smeared her blood on the door frame leading to the bedroom.

Sue fought back, drawing Rick's blood as she struggled. In places, their blood intermingled. The two became one in an ugly, fatal way that mocked and betrayed the vows they had exchanged. Despite her efforts, Sue died that night, beaten to death by the man she once loved.

No one but Richard McFarland—and perhaps his oldest son—know the exact sequence of events that followed his fatal actions. Perhaps he left her body on the love seat that Sue inherited from her mother—it had been against the wall by the bathroom door but was not seen again after that night. Maybe he left her downstairs in the hallway area by the living room in front of a piece of furniture—a bloodstain was found on the floor there and light-colored hairs were caught in the nail of the hinge.

Missing carpet in the white Windstar van indicated that he moved her there at some point. Missing floor mats in the Explorer raised questions about that vehicle as well.

Eventually, Rick did move Sue's body to the two-toned Suburban he had stolen from the Texaco service station. Her presence in that vehicle was apparent. DNA testing proved that her blood was on one floor mat. Forcibly removed strands of her hair were on another.

July 1969 — Beaufort, South Carolina. Sue at 10 1/2 years old with her niece Jenny and her Uncle Bill. *Courtesy Ann Smith Carr*

Sue at 15 in St. Louis. *Courtesy Ann Smith Carr*

1976—Ann's house in St. Louis. Jenny, Huck Smith, Sue at age 17, and Ann. *Courtesy Ann Smith Carr*

Sue in 1977 at William Woods College. *Courtesy Ann Smith Carr*

Sue (*right*) with sorority friends in 1977. *Courtesy Ann Smith Carr*

January 15, 1985 — Sue at Ann's wedding to Gary Carr, with her mother, Mary Elizabeth Smith. *Courtesy Ann Smith Carr*

August 19, 1989 — Sue's wedding to Rick at Webster Grove Presbyterian Church (*l to r*): Ann, Huck, Sue. *Courtesy Ann Smith Carr*

1991—Oxford, Mississippi, at a family funeral. Sue with two-week-old William. *Courtesy Ann Smith Carr*

Sue and Rick with Kirsten, her boyfriend, and the bartender at a bar in Cape Cod, 1991. *Courtesy Kristen Smith*

Sue with William on a Cape Cod Beach in 1991. *Courtesy Kristen Smith*

Mary Elizabeth's 80th birthday in April 1999—at the family plot in St. Peter's Cemetery in Oxford, Mississippi (*l to r*): Ann, Mary Elizabeth, Sue. *Courtesy Ann Smith Carr*

Christmas 2001 in St. Louis. Sue gathered with other family members at Mary Elizabeth's house while she was in the hospital. *Courtesy Ann Smith Carr*

The gracious home where Susan McFarland lost her life. *Photo by Diane Fanning*

The side, garage and back yard of the McFarland home in Terrell Hills with Susan's car parked in the driveway. *Photo by Diane Fanning*

The abandoned farm in rural Bexar County where Richard McFarland burned the body of his wife, Susan. *Courtesy Texas Department of Public Safety*

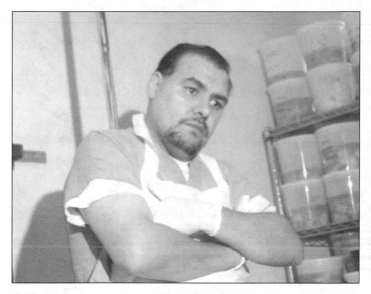

Martin Castillo, Forensic Autopsy Technician at the Bexar County Medical Examiner's Office, takes his first look at the charred remains of Susan McFarland in the autopsy suite in San Antonio. *Courtesy Terrell Hills Police Department*

Ana, the cat belonging to the oldest of the three McFarland boys, rubs on a pot on the porch at 351 Arcadia Place. *Photo by Diane Fanning*

Christmas 2004—at Sue's grave. *Courtesy Ann Smith Carr*

22

Sally the dog was in the McFarlands' front yard. When Susan Schooling stepped outside, she spoke to her, but was not greeted by Sally's usual exuberance. Back inside, Susan said, "Mom, Sally just looked at me and she looked so sad."

A little while later, Charlene let her dogs out. Within minutes a cacophonous barking fest began. Charlene stepped out to quiet them. While she scolded her pets, the front door of the McFarlands' house cracked open. Rick stuck his head outside.

"Hi, Rick. Sorry about the dogs."

Rick popped his head back inside the door without saying a word.

At 10:30, the phone rang at the Matthews home. Rick told Bill that Sue went out with a bunch of stuff to drop off and asked if he had seen her. Then Rick called Blanca. He told her that he had loaded up Sue's car and she had not gotten back yet. "Is she at your house?"

Around 1:30 to 2:00 that morning, Charlene and Susan Schooling were out walking their dogs. They noticed the rear and side doors of the white van were all wide open and Rick was rolling a Shop-Vac from the car to the house. After their walk, Charlene and Susan made a run to Wal-Mart. They returned home at 4 A.M. From the skylight in Sue's bathroom, light streaked into the night sky. They thought it odd, at the time. Sue always went to bed early.

Susan obsessed about the light to the point of irritating her mother. "If you are so worried about it, go knock on the door and ask," Charlene said.

In the days to come, they wished Susan had knocked on that door—it might have spared Sue's family the agony of a prolonged search.

On Tuesday morning, at 7:27, Rick called Sue's work phone. "Susan, Rick," he began as usual. "Did you get up real early this morning? I went to bed at four-forty-five, and you still hadn't come back, so I don't know if you were partying with Margot for her birthday or what. Give me a call when you get in and on my cell. Thanks."

At 7:45, Margot's daughter Ellen looked outside and saw Sue's Ford Explorer parked across from the house. She also saw Rick walking down the street away from it. She said nothing to her mother.

Margot took the kids to school, then she and her friend Tom hit the road on a special mission. Tom wanted to go to Crawford, Texas, to get his picture shot in front of the convenience store George W. Bush patronized when he was in his Texas White House. They were on a tight time schedule—mapquest.com told them the trip was three and a half hours each way—and they needed to get there and back before the kids got out of school.

Just south of Austin, Margot's cell phone rang. It was Rick McFarland. "Did you get my messages?" he asked.

"What messages?"

"I left you messages last night at home and on your cell phone."

"Oh, I went to bed early," Margot said, then paused waiting for Rick to tell her about the messages. He didn't say a word. "What were the messages, Rick?" she asked—impatience sharpening the edges of her words.

"I called you at ten-fifteen because I couldn't find Susan."

That's odd, Margot thought. He'd never wondered about Sue's whereabouts before.

"She went out and never came back," Rick continued.

"Well, what was she doing, Rick?"

"She had me load up the car with stuff and she was running errands."

"Where was she running errands at that time of night?" Margot asked.

"Well, she had a bottle of wine. I thought maybe she was sharing a birthday bottle with you."

"Rick? How did the kids get to school this morning?"

"What do you mean?"

Margot blew out a hard breath of frustration. "Did the kids take the bus? Did you take the kids to school? Did Sue drop them off?"

"Oh. They took the bus."

"Did you call Sue's work?"

"Well, I called and left a message, but she didn't return my call."

"Why don't you call her supervisor—who she reports to?"

"Well, okay. I'll do that."

After she hung up, Margot turned to Tom. "That is the weirdest phone call I ever had." She then called the school to check up on the kids. None of the boys were at school. Sue must have taken them to Amarillo or Houston or St. Louis, she thought.

At 8 A.M., Blanca Hernandez called Sue's work phone: "So where were you last night at ten-thirty? Call me." Blanca was relieved—Sue had recorded a new message, so she must have changed the password.

The next message was from Margot Cromack. "Hey, Susan, it's Margot. Could you give me a call back on the cell when you get back? Talk to ya soon. Bye."

Rick took Timmy to school—but he was running late again. He stopped by the nurse's office to get a tardy slip. Timmy was wearing only one shoe. The nurse sent him to get a pair in the clinic. Rick had blood on his ear and scratches on his face. He said he'd been running and taken a spill. He didn't have his wallet to pay for the shoes.

An hour later, it was Molly Matthews' turn to call Sue. "Susan, this is Molly. Where— I'm wondering where you are. Please give us a call. We're worried about you. Rick had called us last night looking for you, so give me a call. I'm on my way to work and I can be reached on my cell. I'll talk to you later. Bye."

At 10:40, Rick called Sue's work number again. "Susan, Rick. I wish you'd call on the cell. I'm getting sandpaper for buffing the hardwood floors so we can get started on that. Please give a call as soon as possible. Thanks."

At 11 A.M., one of Sue's co-workers thought she had seen Sue by the elevator early in the morning. But when she went to Sue's office later that day to get a signature on a document, Sue was not there.

Real estate agent Deborah Myers was at the Wellses' house, across the street from the McFarlands'. At 11:45, Rick came over, wringing his hands and apologizing for parking his minivan in the driveway. "Is it going to be in your way?"

"No," she told him. "I'm not going to be using the back door."

"What is the new owner going to do with the house? Is it really going to be bulldozed?"

When she told him that was the plan, he asked her if the garage would be bulldozed, too. "Why don't you talk to Harriet? She'll be here any minute now," Deborah said.

Rick's nervousness at that suggestion was obvious. He scurried back across the street and into his own home.

A little later, Harriet Wells arrived at the house. Deborah told her about her encounter with Rick. "It is unusual that he would park in this driveway, but he is an unusual man."

Rick called Betty Saenz, one of Sue's co-workers, with the claim that he was looking for Susan. Betty said she had not seen Sue that day, but another employee had.

Rick giggled. "Oh, someone saw her?"

"Yes."

"I'll keep trying to reach her then." At 4:15, he recorded another message on Sue's voicemail at work, "Susan, Rick. Please give me a call."

On the way back from Crawford, Margot called Rick. "Did you talk to Susan?" she asked, but got no response. "Did you talk to who she reports to?"

Rick stammered, not seeming to understand the questions at all.

"Remember, Rick? We talked earlier today," she said, and then refreshed his memory about their conversation.

"Oh, yeah, right," he said. "I'll call them right away."

On the other side of the Schooling house was the home of Richard and Mimi Riley. Their two daughters were grown and out on their own, making the residence a lot quieter than the boy-filled dwelling two doors up. Marvin the cat appreciated this difference and often wandered up to the Riley house for some solitude. At times, when the boys carried him home, Marvin made a beeline back to the Rileys' the moment he was out of their arms.

Mimi, a third grade teacher, was home from work late Tuesday afternoon when Rick McFarland dropped by.

"I wanted to talk to Richard about the cat."

As Mimi explained that her husband was not home from work, Rick's cell phone rang.

"Hi, Susan," he said. "I'm down here talking to Mimi about Marvin."

At the time, Mimi thought nothing of the call—she did not yet know that Sue was missing.

On Wednesday, November 27, around 4 A.M., Susan Schooling went out to her car. She saw Sue McFarland's Ford Explorer backing out of the driveway and heading west. How strange, she thought, to see Sue's car leaving at this hour. Sue always went to bed at 9:30 and got up at 5. She wouldn't have been surprised to see Rick's car on the road at this time, because he was such a night owl. But Sue?

Margot called Rick that morning and asked, "Have you heard from Susan?"

"No."

"Do you think she went to Amarillo with the boys?"

"I don't know." Rick still allowed Margot to believe the boys were not with him.

"Have you called Amarillo?" she asked, but Rick did not respond. "Did you call Ann?"

"Yes, but you know how those girls like to shop. I just left a message."

"Rick, are you telling me that you guys would travel that far with the kids and not call each other to let the other one know you got there safe?"

Rick did not respond.

"Your relationship is in worse shape than I thought," Margot added.

Once again, Rick had nothing to say. Thinking he would be all alone on Thanksgiving Day, Margot took pity on him. "Why don't you come over our house for Thanksgiving?"

"I've got plans with friends," he said.

Dee Ann Dowlen called Sue that afternoon at 2:15. "Susan, this is Dee Ann and I was just calling to say Happy Thanksgiving, and we're still wanting you to come up here. Talk to you later or after Thanksgiving. Bye-bye."

Out in southeast rural Bexar County, Gil Medillin observed the frequent passage of two unknown vehicles that week—a two-toned Suburban and a black SUV. He tried to wave down the SUV one night, but the driver would not stop. On Wednesday, he saw smoke rising from near an abandoned farmhouse. He did not connect the incidents.

That afternoon, a nervous-sounding man called Little Caesars Pizza on Austin Highway and placed an order for three cheese pizzas for delivery to 351 Arcadia. Arthur Pena made the delivery just after 5:30. A small boy answered the door.

"Is your mom or dad here?" Pena asked.

"My dad is," he said and called out for him several times.

At the top of the stairs across from the front door, Rick McFarland appeared in a pair of clear surgical gloves. As he walked down the steps, Pena told him he had a pizza for him.

"My wife must have ordered it. I didn't," he said. Then, Rick wandered back and forth on the first floor and then up to the second in a search for money. "I have a credit card," he finally told Pena.

"I don't have a machine, but we can call Little Caesars and give them the number." Pena followed Rick through the dining room and into the kitchen to make the call. But the phone was not in the cradle. Rick pushed a button to set the phone off. When it chirped, one of the boys found it down in the sofa cushions and brought it to his dad.

Rick handed the phone to Pena, saying, "I can't dial with these gloves on."

Pena dialed the number and handed the phone back to Rick. After the call, Rick said, "I have to have the receipt. Bring it back to me and I'll give you a big tip—four or five dollars."

Pena insisted that was not necessary, but Rick persisted, saying, "I have to have that receipt."

After making several other deliveries, Pena returned to 351 Arcadia a little after 8:30. Again, one of the boys answered the door and yelled for his dad. Rick appeared once more at the top of the stairs and closed the door behind him before descending. Still in surgical gloves, he signed the receipt and gave Pena a $3 tip.

That same night, at 1 A.M., southeast Bexar County resident Raul Ruiz returned home from the motorcycle races at River City Raceway near Seguin. Driving down South W.W. White Road, he noticed a Suburban parked out in front of an old farmhouse. From a distance, the person with the car looked like a skinhead—maybe one of those kids stealing motorcycles in the area, he thought.

Ruiz slowed his car and rolled down the window. When he stopped, he realized it was not a teenager. It was a middle-aged man with a crew cut and a receding hairline standing holding out a dark bag in the direction of the trees. He thought he'd ask the man if he needed help. But then the man turned his head in Ruiz's direction. The expression on his face was strange and inexplicable. Startled, Ruiz drove away.

One of those sightings marked the night that Rick McFarland drove the stolen Suburban east on Arcadia Place to Burr Duval and headed north to Grandview. He followed that road to Rittiman and then headed south until he reached Interstate 35. In a short while, he veered left off the highway onto Loop 410 where he exited on W.W. White Road.

It was a journey of 15.2 miles to the dreary spot where he abandoned the body of his wife—the mother of his three children—in a rusty, makeshift trailer on the bleak side of town.

Another of these sightings coincided with the return trip he made to set her body on fire. Did he go alone on his funeral pyre excursion? Or did he, as he so often had, leave William and James home alone and take Timmy along for the ride? If Timmy was with him, surely Rick left him in the vehicle while he set the match to obscure Sue's identity. What could Rick have said to him? "Wait here, Timmy, I need to burn some trash"? The possibility that this scenario did occur is real. The horror of it is overwhelming.

Moments before 3 A.M. early Thanksgiving morning, Corporal Joseph Piccolella of the Terrell Hills Police Department was on patrol when he spotted a 1997 Black Eddie Bauer edition Ford Explorer parked in an empty lot on Lazy Lane. He parked directly behind it—he assumed he'd stumbled across a couple of teenagers making out. He used his alley light and the high beams on his police car to brighten the interior of the Explorer, but no heads popped up—there was no movement inside at all. He approached slowly with his flashlight and noticed the vehicle was unlocked and no one was inside. He placed his hand on the hood—it was cold to the touch. He pointed his flashlight at the bushes to see if an amorous couple cuddled in the greenery. No one.

He called in the plates. The vehicle was registered to Richard and Susan McFarland at nearby 351 Arcadia Place. He opened the driver's door and spotted a key in the ignition. He removed the keys and secured the SUV by clicking the lock control device on the key chain. He contacted Dispatch and asked them to find out if the owners were aware of the location of their car.

The dispatcher called 351 Arcadia and Rick answered. "I have an officer with Terrell Hills out with your vehicle on an empty lot at the end of Lazy Lane."

Rick sounded surprised and asked where Lazy Lane was.

"It's in Terrell Hills, right off Ivy Lane."

"It's in Terrell Hills?" Rick said.

"Yes."

"Not—not—uh . . ."

"Alamo Heights?" the dispatcher offered.

"Amarillo, Texas?"

"Amarillo, Texas?"

"Yeah," Rick said, "that's where my wife is supposed to be. It's supposed to be in Amarillo, Texas."

"It is?"

"Yeah."

After informing the officer of this exchange, the dispatcher called Rick again. "Sorry to call you back. The officer's wondering if you're gonna be able to go out there or . . ."

"Yeah, yeah. I mean, don't let him stand out there. I'm trying to get hold of this other party. That's why I didn't call you back yet." Rick then asked a series of questions attempting to pin down the exact location of the Explorer. Then he asked what the officer was planning to do.

The dispatcher put him on hold and checked with Officer Piccolella. When she returned to Rick, she said, "Okay, um, he can either wait on you . . ."

Rick interrupted, "I'll tell you what—just have him bring the keys in, 'cause I've got to wait for this phone call."

"Okay. So have him bring the . . ."

"Bring— Bring— Bring the keys into the station and I'll drive out there and look at it, so he's not, you know, standing there looking at the stars and I'm waiting for this phone call."

"Okay," the dispatcher said.

"Um. So, it's off of Ivy, it's on La— Lazy—Lane and it's located . . ."

"It's in an empty lot."

"In a lot? In an empty lot?" Rick asked.

"Yes, sir."

"Okay. Just have him bring the keys in the station and I'll look at the car and come to the station."

"If not, he said he can take the keys to your residence," the dispatcher suggested.

"No, don't do that. I'm— I'm gonna— Uh— Uh— I'll— I'll go . . ."

"Just take them to the station?"

"Let's just say I'll pick them up at the station," Rick said.

"Okay."

"I'll pick them up at the station. Thanks a lot."

Piccolella left the keys on Corporal Homer Delgado's desk at the Terrell Hills Police Department. Delgado waited—and waited—for Rick McFarland to pick them up.

23

Early Thanksgiving morning, Charlene Schooling awoke to an annoying sound. She got up and peered out her windows and listened. Not a lawnmower. Not a trimmer. It was a circular saw, she thought. And it's coming from the McFarland house.

Charlene didn't know it at the time, but she was probably hearing the sound of Rick cutting up the love seat that sat in the master bedroom on the wall next to the bath. The discovery of charred springs in the trailer with Susan's body made it a possible scenario. Did Rick destroy it because Sue was so fond of it? Or because he never cared for it? Or did it need to be obliterated because it was covered with evidence of a violent attack three nights before?

The love seat—a legacy from Sue's mother—was never seen again after that day. Before Sue disappeared, it was her favorite spot to sit and read stories to her boys before they went to bed.

When Wesley Miller went over to the McFarland house to jump on the trampoline, his mother, Carrie, told him to come back in five minutes. "We have family Thanksgiving things to do and the McFarlands do, too," she said.

When Wesley did not return as instructed, Carrie sent her teenage son Billy over to get him. The front door was answered by Timmy. Inside, the house was dark and gloomy. Timmy yelled for Wesley, but got no answer.

Rick McFarland—in blue jeans and no shirt—opened

a door at the top of the stairs and said, "The kids are playing in the backyard." Then he stepped back into the room and closed the door behind him.

Billy went around back and asked William what his family was doing for Thanksgiving.

"Nothing," William said.

Wesley wanted to bring James home with him for Thanksgiving dinner. Billy told him he couldn't, then took his little brother home.

That afternoon, Rick called Dee Ann Dowlen's cell phone. "Who is this?" he asked.

"It's Dee Ann Dowlen, Rick."

"Oh, happy Thanksgiving. I thought this was George's phone," he said. Then he went on to explain that he was setting up his phone book on his DSL. He was getting the DSL going because Susan didn't like not having a computer at home. Switching subjects, he asked, "Thank you for the three cheese pizzas from Little Caesars."

"Rick, why would I send you pizzas for Thanksgiving?"

"I don't know. It said 'Happy Thanksgiving' on it and I thought it was from you. The pizzas came on Tuesday."

Wanting to end this nonsensical train of conversation, Dee Ann asked, "How is your Thanksgiving going?"

"Kind of funky. The pizzas came on Wednesday. Could I speak to Susan?"

"Rick, you know Susan's not here."

"She wasn't here, so I thought she might have come up there. William said she was going to Amarillo."

"The kids are with you, right?"

"Yeah. I'm just hanging out with the boys."

"Susan wouldn't come without the boys. She cancelled her plans to come to Amarillo on Monday," Dee Ann said.

"What do you think is going on with Susan?"

"I'm not the person you should be talking to about this, Rick." Dee Ann balked at giving any other response, because she did not know if Susan had told Rick about her divorce plans or not.

• • •

It was almost 6 P.M.—nearly fifteen hours after being informed of the discovery of his wife's car in a vacant lot—before Rick managed to show up at the police station to file a missing persons report. He was wearing white canvas work gloves—they appeared brand new—and a long-sleeved jacket.

He told Corporal Delgado that his wife was supposed to be in Amarillo on Monday. Later in the conversation, he contradicted himself, saying that Susan told him on Monday that she would be going to Amarillo later in the week. The last time he saw her, Rick said, was at 9:30 on Monday night when she left the house to deliver gifts to friends in the area. He claimed she never came home that night and he had not seen her since.

It struck Delgado as quite odd that three nights had passed without Rick making any effort to locate his wife. Rick then claimed that he'd jogged to the area where Piccolella told him where he could locate the car, but was unable to find it. Delgado led the way to the Explorer as Rick followed him in his Windstar van. As Delgado approached the area on Lazy Lane, he realized Susan's SUV was in plain view—in the exact location that Piccolella described. He did not believe a jogging man could have run down this way and not seen the vehicle.

Delgado looked at the Explorer and saw a wingback chair, several plastic storage bins, a child's car seat, a gift basket and other items inside, but did not see any obvious signs of foul play. Rick stood in the lot some distance from his wife's car and stared for ten minutes. He never made a move to approach the vehicle. Then he said, "I have three young children at home and I want to go home and care for them." Delgado said he would call him at home if anything was found.

When Delgado called he said he would like to visit Rick. Rick insisted that he did not want any police coming to his home. He'd come by the police station the next day. Rick did not ask if his wife had been found and expressed no interest in any clues or leads the police might have uncovered.

As soon as he got off of the phone, Rick went through the house turning off all of the lights.

That night, Delgado called his friend Charlene Schooling. "Do you have some time to gossip?"

"About what?"

"Your neighbors."

"Which ones?"

"The McFarlands."

"Oh, him," Charlene said in a derisive tone.

"No. Her."

"Susan?"

"Yeah. She's missing."

"What do you mean, missing?"

"Rick reported her missing this evening."

"What?"

"We thought she was in Amarillo, but we found her car off Ivy Lane."

"What?"

"The key was in the ignition."

"What?"

"And the car was unlocked."

"Where are the boys?" Charlene asked.

"With Rick."

"Something is wrong. She would not have gone without the boys."

About 2 A.M., Piccolella picked up Charlene and took her down Ivy Lane to Lazy Lane to Sue's Ford Explorer. Charlene walked around the vehicle and peered through the windows explaining what she recognized and what struck her as odd.

"He's done something with her," she said after her inspection. "Do not let him have this car."

"We've already made arrangements for him to pick up the keys tomorrow."

"Do not let him have those keys. Please. Something is wrong here."

24

November 29, 2002. The day after Thanksgiving. Unlike every other Thanksgiving Friday since she'd lived in Texas, Sue McFarland did not rise at 5 A.M. and dress in the dark. She did not scurry out of the house to make her annual pilgrimage to Toys "R" Us for the after-Thanksgiving sale. She did not fight her way through crowds with a good friend by her side guarding her cart from other desperate shoppers.

Only one person knew why Sue had missed her bargain-hunting ritual. He did not share his insight with anyone.

At 7 A.M., Officer Mitchell from the Terrell Hills Police Department knocked on the Cromacks' front door. Since it was a holiday weekend, everyone was still in bed. Margot invited him in and listened while he explained that he was looking for Sue McFarland.

"Sue's very independent," she told him. "I'm sure she and the boys will be fine."

Margot saw a strange look wash over the policeman's face. "The boys?" he asked.

"Yes. Her boys. She wouldn't go anywhere without her boys."

"The boys have been home all week with Rick."

Alarms rang in Margot's head. Sue did not trust Rick with the kids alone. Then Officer Mitchell told her that they'd found Sue's car just a short distance from her home.

The warning blares were so loud in Margot's head now, she could barely hear anything else the policeman had to say.

As soon as he left, she made a beeline for Arcadia Place. She found Rick at home with his three sons. William told Margot that his dad had cut his finger. When Rick came downstairs, he was wearing gloves on both hands. Margot asked to see his injury, but Rick refused to take off the gloves.

Rick told her he was upset because the police wanted to go through the house.

"The police can come in and look in Sue's closet and figure out if she took off on a trip or what happened to her. If you've done nothing wrong, you have nothing to fear. They can help you."

Rick continued to express discomfort over allowing them into the house, now claiming he was concerned about the boys.

Margot wanted nothing more than an excuse to get the boys away from Rick, and here it was. "Why don't you let me take the boys while you let the cops in your house?"

"I'll think about it," Rick said.

Over at the Miller house, Carrie asked the visiting William McFarland what his family did for Thanksgiving.

"Nothing," William said.

"I haven't seen your mom lately."

"She's in Amarillo on a business trip."

In Amarillo, Dee Ann Dowlen called Rick that morning to ask about Sue. Rick said he had not seen her since Monday and offered no additional information. A little while later, she called again. Unease settled over her like a storm cloud. The greeting on the home phone voicemail was changed. It now said: "This is DOTNETA Partners. Rick McFarland's office."

At 10:30 A.M., daytime patrol officer Sergeant Rick Trevino went to Lazy Lane to confirm that the black Ford Explorer was still there. He opened the front door on the passenger's side and saw a suspicious spot of red on the console between the seats. He called in an impound order.

Alamo Wrecker Service hauled the SUV to the Terrell Hills Police Department, where it was wrapped with yellow crime-scene tape. Then it was towed to the authorized storage facility.

After seeing to Sue's car, Sergeant Trevino went to 351 Arcadia Place, where the front door was answered by Wesley Miller. "Is your dad here?"

"I am not the son in this house. This is my friend's house and I don't know if he's still here," Wesley said, then went upstairs to search, but could not find Rick.

James was at the front door when Wesley came down the stairs. Trevino asked James to go get his mother.

"You can't disturb her," he said. "She is in a very deep sleep."

"Then get your dad."

"He's asleep, too," James said, but would not go look for his parents.

Soon after Trevino left, Rick was in the living room yelling, "Goddammit! You were supposed to tell him that I went jogging."

Just before 1, Rosa Garcia from My Day Cleaning Service entered 351 Arcadia Place for her weekly house-cleaning assignment. Rick was not at home, but the three boys were there, along with Wesley Miller. As Rosa cleaned, she observed that the house was neater than usual, and she noticed two missing items: the round white trash can from the master bath and the VCR from the master bedroom. But she did not attach any significance to the absence of the items.

Usually when she finished she retrieved a $40 check signed by Susan McFarland from under a magnet on the refrigerator. On this day, there was no check.

Rick stopped by the Terrell Hills police station. When he saw Sergeant Trevino, he asked, "Could this have been a carjacking?"

"Carjackers normally take the vehicle. It is not the norm to carjack someone and then drop the vehicle off only a few blocks from where they live," the officer said. "When the vehicle is found later, it is normally stripped, burned or wrecked, but hardly ever with the keys left in it. If this was a case of carjacking, whoever did it was stupid and careless."

Rick said nothing, but appeared incensed at Trevino's comments as he left the station.

Trevino called Amarillo to see if he could get any information from Dee Ann Dowlen. He told her he was investigating a missing persons report filed by Richard McFarland. After establishing that she had no idea of Sue's location, Dee Ann asked, "Don't you know she has a large family?"

"I just know that her mother and father are dead," Trevino said. For some reason, that was the only information about Sue's family that Rick shared.

"She has brothers, a sister, nieces, nephews and cousins in Missouri," Dee Ann said, and gave him Ann Carr's phone number.

When Trevino presented all of this information to the investigating officer, it was decision time for Detective Sergeant Boyd Wedding. There was possible blood in the missing woman's car. Terrell Hills did not have a crime lab. This case had the potential for being bigger than any ever handled by the men at the department. They'd had a murder in June, but before that, there had not been a homicide in Terrell Hills in ten years. The thirteen-person department handled two robberies—neither one armed—thirty-four burglaries and no rapes in the previous year. It was one of the safest communities for miles and as such, the police department was inexperienced in serious crime.

If Sue McFarland was dead, the Terrell Hills Police Department needed help to put the perpetrator behind bars. Wedding was not too proud to ask. He called Texas Ranger Shawn Palmer for assistance.

• • •

Dee Ann Dowlen started the day concerned about her friend Sue. The call from the police elevated her worry to alarm. She called Rick again and demanded to know what was going on.

"Rick," Dee Ann said, "when was the last time you saw Sue?"

"She got up early for work on Tuesday. When I called there, someone told me she just left."

"How could you not tell me that she's missing?"

"Well, there's this little deal where they found the car," he said.

"What are you talking about, Rick?"

"The police found Susan's car."

"Where?"

"A couple of blocks from here."

"Then why the hell did you think she was in Amarillo?"

"It was probably a mugger, because of the missing electronic equipment."

"What kind of equipment?" Dee Ann asked.

"DVDs and VCRs," Rick said. "Do you think Susan has a boyfriend?"

"What?"

"I read in this book that they always blame it on the husband."

"Blame what on the husband?"

"The book said that the husband is always a suspect."

"What book are you talking about, Rick?"

"Some book I read in college."

"I'm calling Sue's sister right now," a shaken Dee Ann said and hung up the phone.

Rick decided he'd better be the first to call Ann. "Do you know where Susan is?" he asked.

"What do you mean, do I know where Susan is?" Ann gestured to her husband to pick up the other phone.

"Do you think . . . Do you know . . . Do you think she would . . ." Rick stammered.

"What are you asking me, Rick?"

"Do you think she would go off?"

"Are you trying to ask me if Sue is having an affair?"

"Yes."

"Absolutely not. She does not have time for an affair. She has to work a job," Ann snapped.

Rick mumbled incoherently.

"Rick, put Sue on the phone."

"I don't know where Susan is now," he said, then mumbled something indistinct that sounded as if he wanted to get off the line.

"Don't hang up the phone, Rick," Ann ordered.

"I got to go now," Rick replied and ended the call.

Ann and her husband talked about the bizarre conversation. They had more questions than answers. Then, they got a call from Dee Ann, who related the conversation from her phone call with Rick.

When Ann got off of the phone, she called both of her brothers. Then she thought that it would be courteous to call the elder McFarlands also. When she informed Mona of the situation, the response she received stunned her.

"We know Susan disappeared," Mona said. "We think she is having an affair."

Harley Smith, Sue's oldest brother, placed a call to his daughter. Kirsten was in the parking lot of Tuesday Morning, one of Sue's favorite shops, when her cell phone rang. Harley told Kirsten that Sue was missing. Like the rest of the family, Kirsten was surprised, confused and concerned.

Rick next called Blanca Hernandez and told her about the discovery of Sue's car, then asked, "Do you think Susan is having a rendezvous?"

"I think Sue might have needed some time," Blanca said.

"Something bad must have happened, and the husband is always a suspect. Could you tell the boys about Susan's disappearance?"

Blanca advised him to call William's psychiatrist.

. . .

About 3 P.M., Rick called the Matthews home. Bill answered and Rick asked to speak to Molly. When Bill said she was not there, Rick asked, "When was the last time you saw Susan?"

"What's going on, Rick?"

"Susan's missing. Her car has been found in a field off Lazy Lane with the keys inside."

"Did you call the police?"

"They called me when they found the car. When she left the house, she had two DVDs, a thirteen-inch television and a shiny new laptop in the back of the car. They're not there now."

"Where are the boys?"

"They're with me."

That simple sentence shattered the Matthewses' illusion that all was well. It destroyed their theory that Sue had packed up the kids and hauled out to Amarillo and just wasn't in the mood to talk to anyone. Something was wrong. They knew that without a doubt. But the thought that Rick was responsible never crossed their minds.

Bill suggested actions Rick could take to help locate his wife—like going on line to determine credit card activity. But Rick did not seem interested in doing anything to track her down.

25

Across the street from the McFarlands', Harriet Wells dropped by her house, which was now up for sale. Her new home was nearby, keeping her connected to the neighborhood grapevine. As was her usual practice, she pulled into the rear driveway where her comings and goings would be out of sight of Rick McFarland.

She approached the back door and out of the corner of her eye, caught a glimpse of something not quite right through the garage window. She opened the door to the garage and discovered a blue-and-gray Suburban with its windows all rolled down parked inside. Harriet was stunned—whoever had parked the car needed to do three things first: come inside her gate, go into the garage and activate the door opener. After that, the intruder had to move the old couch where the dogs used to sleep and relocate a table and a few other items to make enough room to be able to shut the door behind the large vehicle. She knew the McFarlands did not own a Suburban. Still, the first thought was: What has Rick done now?

Harriet suspected McFarland, but did not know with certainty—she wanted proof. She climbed in and searched the Suburban for clues. She came up empty in the obvious places—the console area and the glove compartment. In the back seat, she spotted a brand new Christmas sweatshirt and a canvas basket. She reached into the container and pulled out a clear plastic folder. Inside, she found an AAA card and a credit card—both bearing Richard McFarland's name. She put everything back where she found it and exited the car.

Coming around the side, she saw other alien items in her garage—one large and two small gasoline containers, two bottles of insecticide, two big bags of charcoal, a roll of paper towels and a half-empty bottle of orange cleanser. She had never seen any of these things before. In fact, when she was at the house the day before, none of it was present—not even the Suburban.

She looked over the charcoal and gasoline again. Her eyes widened at the thought that raced through her mind: He's killed her, cut up her body and burned it.

She called her husband, Ned, and told him about what she'd found and what she suspected.

"Let me call Rick," he said.

"No, I don't want to mess with him," Harriet said.

"Then call the police."

"Okay. But first I want to get done what I came here to do." Harriet took care of her planned chores and then called the Terrell Hills Police Department and reported the presence of a strange vehicle in her garage.

Across the street, other police officers posted on the street knocked on the McFarland front door. They knew Rick was inside, but they got no response. They went next door to the Schooling house and asked Charlene if they could come inside and keep an eye on her neighbor's house. They wanted to catch Rick if he came out.

About a half hour later Rick emerged in bright orange wind pants and a white tee shirt. He raced to his car, jumped in and tore out of the driveway. The officers dashed out Charlene's front door and took off after him.

Twenty minutes later, Rick pulled into his driveway and the police car parked across the street. Rick went into his garage and came out with an orange power cord, which he unwrapped with methodical care and stretched back to the garage. He returned with a circular saw in hand. He plugged it into the end of the cord, started it up and proceeded to score a line across his driveway.

When he finished, he put his tools away and walked across the street to Harriet's house. At this point, a fascinated Charlene lost sight of him from her windows. She kept looking out, intrigued by what might happen next. She was so captivated by the odd behavior she was witnessing that she ignored her telephone when it rang.

Officers Delgado and Trevino had arrived at 356 Arcadia by now. They saw this strange performance, too, along with Harriet Wells. Delgado turned to Harriet and said, "Ma'am, his wife is missing."

That was enough to convince Harriet that the purpose of the cutting of the pavement in the driveway was to heat up the blade enough to destroy any evidence on it.

In the garage, Harriet and the police watched Rick as he watched them—walking back and forth in front of them with a false air of nonchalance. Charlene couldn't see this routine, but she kept watch, and in two or three minutes was rewarded when James came out the front door and crossed the street with a portable phone receiver in hand.

As James handed the phone to his dad, Harriet and Trevino locked eyes. Rick turned and walked away.

Once again, Rick was in Charlene's sights—walking back across the street talking on the phone. When he went inside, Charlene checked her voice mail. There was an urgent message from Harriet Wells pleading with her to call right away. When she did, Harriet told her about the strange car in the garage, and that Officers Trevino and Delgado were there to investigate, and wanted Charlene to come over to see if she recognized the vehicle.

Charlene was reluctant to walk across the street in clear view of Rick McFarland. Instead, she got into her car, drove around the block and approached Harriet's house from the rear. As soon as she walked into the garage, Charlene asked, "What was Rick doing over here?"

"He just walked by and stared at us," Corporal Delgado said.

Charlene did not recognize the Suburban in Harriet's garage and looked at the other items that had mysteriously appeared there. When she saw the can of bug spray, she choked. Because of her experience watching forensic shows on television, she felt certain that Rick had sprayed the area where he'd left Sue's body to keep the bugs away.

"Have you looked under the car for weeds and dirt?" Charlene asked.

When she got a negative response, she got down on her hands and knees and peered up at the undercarriage. From floor level, she hollered up, "Come see all the weeds and mud under here."

As she pushed herself to her feet, her face inches away from the bumper, she and Harriet gasped in unison. There on that bumper was a telltale thumbprint smudge of red. Harriet said, "Officers, that looks like blood to me."

The men looked at the scarlet smear and said, "Sure does. That's blood."

The possibility of a connection to Sue's disappearance was now clear. The officers ran the plate on the Suburban and connected it to a Suburban owned by Ron Zimmerman—a producer for *America's Most Wanted*.

They reported this to Police Chief Larry Semander. Semander called Zimmerman's home and the call transferred to his cell phone. "Do you know where your car is?" Semander asked.

"It's sitting in the driveway."

"No, it's not."

Zimmerman then explained that he was at SeaWorld in San Diego and was sopping wet from a splash he'd just received from Shamu.

Then the word came in that, although the tags belonged to Zimmerman, the Suburban in the Arcadia garage did not. Zimmerman had no idea of how his plates got on another vehicle—but he did offer one clue.

He said that as he was preparing to leave town, he'd stopped by the Texaco service center, where he encountered a man who identified himself as "Ballew" and said he lived on Arcadia. "Ballew" offered to drive him to the airport and return the Suburban to Zimmerman's driveway in Terrell Hills.

Semander relayed this information to Trevino, who shared it with Charlene and Harriet. Charlene asked, "Who do you think 'Ballew' is?"

Trevino jerked his head toward the McFarland house and said, "Probably our friend."

On orders of Chief Semander, Delgado and Trevino secured the garage as a crime scene.

26

Trevino crossed the street to join Detective Sergeant Boyd Wedding. The two officers explained that they were here to investigate the missing persons report and asked Rick to sign a consent form to search the premises. Rick did so without objection and then called Margot to come pick up the kids. While Wedding and Trevino searched, a police officer sat with the boys as they watched television.

About fifteen minutes later, Texas Ranger Shawn Palmer arrived to assist. He introduced himself to Rick McFarland and shook his hand. At that moment, Palmer sensed that Sue McFarland was dead and that the hand he held in his was the one that killed her.

Palmer and Wedding went upstairs to examine the master bedroom and bath. Palmer discovered what appeared to be blood droplets five feet above the floor on the wall in the master bath along with other stains and smears that looked consistent with blood.

The men went downstairs and Palmer went outside. He looked through the window of the white Windstar van parked in the driveway. There was no carpeting on the floor.

Margot answered Rick's call for assistance and pulled up at the house at 7:15. She was shocked by the chaos before her eyes. Flashing, spinning lights lit the night sky and police swarmed everywhere. She went up to the back door and an officer told her, "Ma'am, you cannot go inside."

The boys came to the door and she told them to go get

their shoes, jackets and some books. Then she told the officer, "I need to talk to Rick before I leave, because I need to know what he's told the boys. I need to know where to start."

James and Timmy came out of the house and said that William was not there. As she got those two situated in the car, a police vehicle with flashing lights pulled up to the house and William bolted out of it. "Where's my mommy? Where's my mommy?" he cried in a panicked voice.

Margot put an arm around him and moved him toward her car. "We don't know where your mommy is. That's why all the police are here. You're going to spend the night at my house so your dad can take care of all of this. So they can find out where your mom is."

She got William into the car and Rick walked up with a garbage bag full of stuff for the boys.

"What did you tell them, Rick?"

"About what?"

"About their mother. About what happened to her."

"I didn't tell them anything."

Margot stuffed down her impatience and got into the car. By the time she checked that all the seat belts were fastened, Rick was back.

"They told me I can't spend the night here. Can I spend the night at your house?"

She wanted to say no, but the boys were listening, and the Cromacks were the closest thing to family they had in San Antonio. Her concern for William, James and Timmy was genuine and deep. She said yes. She did not want Rick in her home, but she feared he would take the boys from her if she did not agree. It was a small price to pay to ensure their well-being.

As soon as Margot and the boys left, Palmer began his first interview with Rick McFarland in the living room of his home. He asked about Sue's friends, her credit and debit cards and whether or not she carried a pager. The interview was punctuated with Rick's loud yawns.

Palmer asked, "Is there anything that you know that she

packed for the trip that would be—should have been—in the car?"

"No."

"Or that she was planning to take?"

McFarland explained about the plastic storage bins that Sue planned on giving away on Monday when she went out. He also said she would have had a TV/VCR, a computer and a laptop in her car.

"Did you happen to see those—I assume they were still in there Monday night?"

"Yeah, yeah," Rick responded.

"Do you know if she came home late and left early that morning to go to work?"

"No, I don't."

"Was there anything to show that, like, maybe she had showered or done something?" Palmer pressed. "'Cause I know you said that you confirmed she was at work."

Palmer questioned Rick about the identity of the person on the other end of the line at Southwestern Bell who told Rick Sue had been seen at work on Tuesday morning, but McFarland said he only knew it was a woman.

"Was there anything to indicate that she'd come home after you'd gone to sleep Monday and gotten up Tuesday and gone to work?"

Rick's response was no more than a mumble.

"Do you all sleep in the same room?" Palmer asked.

Rick wiggled around the question, mumbling all the while, then finally stated his answer clearly, "I was downstairs on the couch."

"It didn't look like she'd slept in the bed?"

"She is real tidy," Rick said, then tripped over incomplete sentences having to do with Sue's obsessive need to make the bed when she arose.

"Was there anything else to indicate that she'd come home and gone to work from here rather than somewhere else?"

"No. I mean, I was assuming that when I called the Dowlens. I had no sense of alarm until she wasn't there. You know when they called and said that her car was found—the

make and model? She had just ordered, uh, uh . . . somebody ordered three cheese pizzas for us Tuesday night and
that was in keeping with activities, so I felt everything was
basically, relatively normal with the things . . ."

Palmer noticed that Rick had abrasions on the knuckles
of his left hand. He also had a section missing from the tip of
the small finger on his right hand. Small red scratches drew
long lines down his neck. Palmer turned the conversation to
Rick's injuries. "You said you cut your finger working?"

"Yeah, with a saw. You know, I was jogging, I ran into a
thorn tree . . ."

"When was that?"

"Uh, what's today? Two days ago. What's today, Friday?"

"Today's Friday," Palmer confirmed.

"I guess Wednesday."

"And that was here at the house?"

"Yeah."

"And your knuckles there in your left hand?" Palmer
asked.

"Uh huh."

"How did that happen?"

"Um, when I fell," Rick said.

"Fell jogging?"

"Yeah."

"When was that?"

"Tuesday, I guess."

"Do you jog every morning, or . . . ?"

"Oh no, I wouldn't say every morning. But maybe twice a
week," Rick said.

As the investigation progressed from this point, Palmer
would ask everyone who knew McFarland about the frequency of his jogging. No one could confirm that he ever
went running.

"When you cut your finger, did you go to the doctor or
anything at all?" Palmer asked.

"No."

"How about when you fell?"

"No."

"No? I guess you took care of yourself here at the house?"

"Yeah."

"I noticed that there was some blood up there in the master bedroom. Do you know where that's from?"

"It could have been a minor incident."

"That's what I'm asking," Palmer persisted. "Did you clean your hands up there in the bathroom when you cut yourself?"

"Yeah."

Palmer switched the topic to the cleaning lady who had been in the house earlier that day. McFarland claimed that My Day Cleaning Service came every Friday. Palmer segued into personal questions about Rick's marriage. "Is there anything unusual with you all's relationship recently? Where she just might up and leave?"

"No. No," Rick denied.

"Were you all having any more problems than usual right now?"

Rick mumbled a response.

"She hadn't talked about wanting to leave?"

"No," Rick insisted, then added, "It's never been discussed before, but . . ."

"Has she ever disappeared before?"

Rick muttered a negative response.

"No? Has she ever left for a day or overnight or anything without letting you know?"

"No."

"No? Do you have any idea where she would have gone?" Palmer asked. "If she decided to leave and didn't want to talk to you, do you have any idea where she would have gone other than the friends you mentioned?"

"No."

"Was she seeing anybody else that you know of? As far as you know, she didn't have a boyfriend or anything?"

"Correct."

Palmer moved his questioning to the van in the driveway. "How long ago did you have the carpet taken out?"

"A week and a half—Wednesday."

"What was wrong with the carpet that you had them take it out?"

"The kids, I guess."

Palmer next asked about the map book he'd seen in the Windstar van and asked Rick why it was there. Rick explained that he used it to try to locate Lazy Lane before he jogged over to look at his wife's car.

Palmer then turned his questions to the house for sale across the street. "Have you ever been in that house before?"

"Yeah," Rick said and added that he had been there for the open house a couple of weeks ago. Palmer asked about parking the Windstar in the driveway there.

Rick claimed he parked it there because of the party and the kids' desire to skateboard in his driveway.

"Have you ever been in the garage over there?"

Rick denied being in the garage until Palmer pinned him in a corner by asking, "Is there any reason why there would be anything of yours in the garage?"

"Huh. I can't think of a reason. It's, uh, I visited there once, when the tank ran out of gas. I put some stuff over there."

"What did you put over there?" Palmer asked.

"We were cleaning out space."

"Well, like, for instance . . . ?"

"There's a storage shelf, cans, bags, charcoal, and, uh, just big stuff, bug stuff," Rick said. Then, after a little back and forth, he added, "I took the liberty of just putting stuff in there till we got it put back."

"You have anything over there right now?"

"We might have some stuff in there."

"Like what?"

"I don't recall."

"I mean, 'cause if they are selling the house, I would guess they probably wouldn't want all that stuff over there."

"Yeah," Rick acknowledged.

"Kind of a mess."

"Yeah."

"So when do you think that you last saw her—you said Monday?" Palmer said, switching subjects again.

"Monday evening."

"Monday evening. And what time do you think that was, did you say?"

"Nine o'clock."

Palmer then moved the discussion to the three little boys. "The kids are both yours and hers?"

Rick nodded his head.

"Have they asked for their mother?"

"They're starting to."

"Are they? When did they start asking for her?"

"Friday. She's still in Amarillo."

Palmer then asked Rick to accompany him to the Terrell Hills Police Department to give a written statement. Rick refused to do so until he had spoken to an attorney. Palmer then informed him that the investigators were seeking a formal search warrant and he would need to vacate the premises.

Palmer then went over to 356 Arcadia Place to take a look at the Suburban in the garage. Among the items he noted in the vehicle were an open twelve-pack of Sprite, a large quantity of Band-Aid packages in plastic shopping bags and a green military-style shovel. Another item of interest was a multi-tool. When it was tested, techs found a mixture of blood was predominately Susan's with a commingling of some blood from Rick. In a bloodstain on one bag of charcoal taken from the garage, they found more of the same DNA combination.

It was impossible to live within a block of 351 Arcadia and not be aware of the police activity there. In no time, the reason for their presence echoed through the neighborhood. When Carrie Miller heard that Sue was missing, she called Melissa St. John.

Melissa did not hesitate before saying, "My God, that makes me sick. He killed her."

27

At 8:15 on the morning of November 30, 2004, the Bexar County Magistrates' Office issued a search warrant for the McFarland home, the Explorer and the Suburban. On the way to Arcadia Place, Wedding and Palmer stopped by the Texaco service center. Station owner Richard Clemmer was not at the station, but an employee showed the officers the board on the wall containing keys—the key to the Suburban hung there on a hook.

They arrived at 351 Arcadia Place at 9 A.M. Roaming around the exterior of the home and into the garage, they shot photographs and looked at anything with possible evidentiary value. At noon, forensic experts from the Texas Department of Public Safety Crime Laboratory Service joined the investigators.

They started their work in the Suburban across the street, swabbing, taking tape lifts and cataloguing the contents of the vehicle—from a military-style shovel to a packet of receipts to empty Wyler's Authentic Italian Ices wrappers.

In the middle of the search, Wedding and Palmer got a call from a patrolman at the Texaco service center. Richard Clemmer said that only one person ever test drove the Suburban. That person wrote a name, Mark Lynn, and a phone number in Clemmer's message pad. The number was phony—they could only assume the name was, too.

Crime lab personnel turned next to the white Ford Windstar

van. On the front passenger seat headrest, they swabbed a suspected bloodstain.

In the house, the forensics team swabbed at every suspicious stain they saw, starting with a spot on the threshold of the side door and moving through the hallway and up the stairs to the master bedroom and bath. Investigators gathered toothbrushes, clothing, tools and latex gloves. From Rick's second-floor office, they confiscated a .380 semi-automatic handgun and a magazine—neither contained any ammunition. On a shelf near the door, Palmer found two wooden boxes filled with Sheffield knives and an assortment of multi-purpose tools.

At a quarter till 8 that evening, the work was done. Palmer left a message for Rick McFarland to that effect. On the table in the family room, he left a copy of the search warrant and an inventory list of the items seized.

The investigative team then proceeded to the impound lot for a thorough search of the Ford Explorer. They documented and bagged every item in Sue's SUV and swabbed all suspected spots of blood. Palmer noted that although there were no floor mats in the car, dimples in the carpet indicated their recent presence there.

In St. Louis, Ann spent a major part of her day on the telephone. She talked to family and friends. She called every Gary Long in the phone book in an attempt to reach Sue's supervisor over the weekend. Late Saturday evening, she finally connected with the right Gary Long.

She also made plans for her departure the next day. She wanted company on the trip, but she also wanted the most appropriate and useful person to come along. She decided on Kirsten—not only was she close to Sue, but, more important, she was close to the boys, and they would need someone they trusted.

Of all the calls Ann made that day, the most disturbing and depressing was the conversation she had with her brother, Pete Smith.

Pete was a retired homicide investigator. He told his sister, "This is bad. This is really bad. It's not going to come out well."

28

Rick was with his children at the Cromacks' house on Elizabeth Road in Terrell Hills. The police posted a team in front to monitor Rick's activity.

When Margot got up Saturday morning, the kids were all gathered around the television, but Rick could not be found anywhere. She went over to 351 Arcadia and asked if Rick McFarland was there, or if the officers knew where he was.

Everyone there thought he was at Margot's house. At some point, early in the morning, out of sight of his spotters, Rick slipped out the back door and was not seen for the rest of the day.

Margot spent the whole day cooking for six hungry kids. She tried to reach Rick without success all day long and into the night.

At 5 A.M. Sunday morning, Rick knocked on the door of a Bible study friend, Attorney Corbin Snow. Rick said he needed a shower and an attorney. Snow had a detached guest house with a kitchen and a bath. He allowed Rick to use it to clean up and take a nap.

Rick left behind the clothes he wearing on November 29—a pair of red wine–colored pants, a pair of boxer shorts and a white pullover shirt. Later, an aluminum Little League baseball bat was found under the bed. The bat was scratched and had a large chip missing out of the end. After a thorough examination, none of these items was of any evidentiary value.

On Sunday, officers released 356 Arcadia and Harriet returned to her house. While she was there, Rick called Ned Wells, saying that he had spoken to their Realtor the week before and now needed her name and phone number.

Ned did not feel in a helpful mood and played dumb. Rick blathered on. "I'm trying to work on my time line."

"Well, Rick, her sign is still in our front yard, you can look out your window and see it."

"No, I can't," Rick said. "I'm at a remote location."

Ned could only shake his head. Remote location? Man, this guy is weird.

Realtor Deborah Mills received several calls from the same number that day. She suspected they were from Rick and, not wanting a repeat of the last strange encounter, did not answer. The caller did not leave any messages.

Ann and Kirsten drove down to San Antonio in the belief that they would return home in a day or two. They were convinced that Sue would show up at work on Monday morning with some incredible tale that would explain the whole mystery.

After all, they had never seen any violence from Rick. They didn't think he had the concentration or creativity to conceive and follow through on a lethal plot. They did not believe that Sue would allow Rick to get the best of her.

29

William told Doug Cromack about the injury on his dad's hand. Doug, a hand surgeon, insisted on looking at it when Rick returned on Sunday. Doug examined the finger with the missing tip, he was surprised at the severity of the wound. He dressed it and gave Rick advice on its care.

On Sunday night, Rick and Margot argued about the boys going back to school. Margot thought it would be good for them to slip back into their normal routine. Rick objected, "People will make fun of them. They need to be with me. They need me."

No matter what Margot said, Rick was adamant.

But the next morning, Rick told her that he would take the boys to school. Margot left the house with her kids, dropped them off and then went to the gym to work out. After that, she went over to her youngest daughter Ellen's school to perform her weekly volunteer duties in the classroom. Ellen was in the same class as James McFarland. When Margot arrived, James was not there. She remembered Sue's long-held fear that one day Rick would grab the kids and take off for parts unknown. Margot flew straight back home.

To her relief, the boys were all in the backyard playing in the treehouse. Was Rick with them? Of course not. He was in the back room of the house talking on the telephone. Margot was furious.

"Rick, have you called your pediatrician?"

"Why should I call my pediatrician?"

"Did you call the psychiatrist?"

"Why?"

Margot was flabbergasted. "Haven't you even thought about getting support or counseling for the boys?"

Rick just shrugged and walked away.

Despite Rick's insistence that the boys needed him and needed to be with him, Rick disappeared with great frequency during his stay at the Cromack home. He wasn't there for meals. He wasn't there to tuck the boys into bed for the night.

Margot urged him to stay at home, but he did not listen. The kids were shattered. She and her husband stood in as best they could. Margot snuggled with them, played games with them and talked to them about everything under the sun. Doug—who as a rule, never made it home from the hospital in time for dinner—left work early each night to eat with the boys and fill the gap created by Rick's absence.

30

On Monday, December 2, investigators arrived at Southwestern Bell Corporation on the Riverwalk in downtown San Antonio. During the search of Sue's work station, they found a time sheet. On it, her vacation time for that week was spelled out—she had planned to leave two hours early on Wednesday, November 27. There was no indication that she did not intend to be at work the Tuesday before that.

The officers listened to Sue's voicemail messages, found documents related to her pending divorce and retrieved the last document entered on her computer. They also brushed against the heart and soul of Sue McFarland—a Disney Cruise Line folder that embodied her love of her children, and a list of books to read that included one prescient title, *The Lovely Bones* by Alice Sebold, the story of a young girl who after her death sat in heaven and followed the lives of her loved ones on earth.

While Sue's office was searched, Ann and Kirsten went to the Terrell Hills Police Department and got an update on the missing persons investigation. They did not pick up on the officers' suspicions about Rick.

Then they went to the Cromack home to visit with the boys and talk to Rick. Timmy was up in the treehouse when they arrived.

He hollered down, "Auntie Ann, Kirsten! Our mom is dead."

"We don't know that," Ann said. "That's why we're here—to help find out what happened to your mom."

When they talked to Rick, Ann tiptoed around her questions hoping to find a logical but indirect and non-offensive path to the information she wanted from her brother-in-law.

Impatient, Kirsten butted in. "Cut to the chase. What the hell happened to her, Rick? What do you think happened to Sue?"

"She went to drop off some things in a not very good neighborhood. She went to drop them off and she was out of her car unloading stuff and she was seen by some Guido in a low-rider," he said. "He came by, hit her on the head, abducted her and had his way with her. She's been carjacked."

Ann and Kirsten noticed the cuts all over Rick's hands and arms. He explained that he had been out jogging and ran into a bush. Then they asked about the missing tip on his little finger. Rick said that he was cutting something with a saw and the saw slipped. Rick then complained that the police weren't doing anything.

"Have you given them permission to check stuff out—to search the house?" Ann asked.

"I'm not sure."

"Well, go down to the police station and find out."

"Ann, would you go with me?"

"Of course."

Since Kirsten wanted to be at the station, too, and Margot needed to leave her house, there was a question about what to do with the boys.

Rick thought it would be fine to leave them at Margot's without adult supervision. The three women vetoed that idea.

Ann and Kirsten went to the Terrell Hills Police Department. Kate Kohl, executive director of the Heidi Search Center, called the station earlier and asked Sergeant Wedding to pass the center's phone number on to the family. Ann and Kirsten did not call. They drove straight over to the center's office in Windsor Park Mall. The staff overwhelmed the two women with the depth of their concern and understanding. "They were a guiding and calming force in a time of desperation, unknowing and fear," Kirsten said.

Later that day, Sue's supervisor, Gary Long, returned a call from Rick McFarland. Rick claimed he wanted to find anyone who had seen Sue on Tuesday. He said, "Until a body is found or Susan shows up, I am the main suspect."

Rick also called Julie Speer. Three times he left voicemail messages. Once he spoke to her husband. Every time, he requested that Julie give him a call. When she finally got back to him, she asked how he was doing.

"Bad," he said. "What did you and Susan talk about?"

"Do you mean what did we talk about when I was there Wednesday?"

"Yes," he said. "Did Susan mention where she would be going?"

"No," Julie said. "Where do you think she might have gone?"

"Susan told me she was going to Amarillo with the boys. Me and the boys are always the last to know Susan's plans."

"What were you going to do when they left?"

"Since Susan is always nagging me about cleaning up the office, I decided to clean it. She harps so much about the office. What was the name of the mechanic you referred Susan to?"

"What are you talking about?"

"Me and Susan were looking at purchasing a car."

"She didn't mention that to me," Julie said.

"She said a friend referred her to a mechanic. I liked a Jeep, but Susan liked a Suburban. So, of course, we were going to get the Suburban."

"I don't know a mechanic that could help with a Suburban."

"What did Susan drop off for you Monday?"

"Susan did not drop anything off."

Rick asked the same question two more times, despite her denial. The conversation was striking a dissonant chord that made Julie uncomfortable. Nothing Rick said felt spontaneous—it was as if he had a list of questions and was checking them off one by one.

"What can you tell me about the chair in the Explorer?" Rick continued.

"What chair?"

"The rocker. Why is it in the Explorer?"

Julie remembered that rocker—the one Sue inherited from her mother. It was broken and Sue had said Rick hated it. "I told her where to have it repaired," Julie said.

On the morning of December 3, Rick, Ann and Kirsten met with the Heidi Search Center staff at the Terrell Hills Police Department for a briefing on the next steps. After that, the search experts got to work.

With a dog team from Greater Bexar Search and Rescue, Kate Kohl and Vanessa Hanes from the center covered the lot on Lazy Lane where the police found Sue's Explorer. While they searched, the ever-efficient Mary Dry kept the phones answered and the center's office opened and operational.

The dogs keyed in on the spot where Sue's vehicle had been parked. This scent did not mean Sue had ever been to that location. It only meant that enough of her smell had drifted from the car when the door was opened for the sensitive noses of the search dogs to recognize it. The canines sniffed every square inch of the lot, but did not stir up any answers. The scent of hope was fading fast in Terrell Hills.

31

At the request of law enforcement, a handful of searchers then went to Holbrook Park, where the McFarland boys had taken horse-riding lessons. They scoured the territory from Eisenhauer Road down to the Fort Sam Houston Army Base.

The search for Susan McFarland was already taking a different path from most of the center's searches. Usually, they started in a small area where the missing person was last seen and slowly expanded the search parameters in a big circle around that spot.

With this effort, however, they jumped around the city following leads from law enforcement and Ann Carr. Often, they sent out small reconnaissance teams to scope out an area for a possible full-blown search.

The day the searching began, Rick stopped by the Texaco service center again. When he pulled up, Richard Clemmer recognized him as the man he'd seen in the news whose wife was missing and said, "I was sorry to hear about your wife."

"Thank you," Rick responded. "Have you talked to the police?"

"No."

"I want to talk to you before you talk to the police. I want to get our stories straight. I did not steal the Suburban. I took it so my wife could check it out. I took it on Saturday after I'd seen you. I want you to tell the police that you gave me the keys."

Rick also requested that Clemmer question the police

about what had been found in the Suburban. Then he said, "The strange thing is that the Suburban has the wrong plates on it. The plates belong to another Suburban. Do you know anything about that?"

"No," said Clemmer.

"If we keep our stories straight, everything will be okay. I'll buy you a steak when this is all over." Rick wrote down his name and phone number. Clemmer knew right away it was not the same one he'd given the week before. He went to the message book to double-check his memory and discovered the message was gone. In fact, the whole page had been ripped from the book.

At 3:45, Richard Clemmer was at the Terrell Hills Police Department telling the whole sequence of events to Palmer and Wedding. He signed a statement and agreed to allow his phone conversations with Rick McFarland to be recorded.

After several fruitless attempts, Clemmer finally reached Rick on his phone at 9:45. "Rick?"

"Yes. It's Richard?"

"Yes, sir. Well, they had me in the hot seat this afternoon," Clemmer said.

"What do you mean, that uh . . ."

"The Terrell Hills Police Department."

"Okay."

"They were grilling me hard . . ."

"Yeah. Okay."

"And, uh, they wanted to know when you picked it up and who all knew about it and stuff like that."

"Uh huh."

"I didn't have the answers because I wasn't there when you picked it up, and that's what I told them."

Rick stammered and stuttered—at a loss for words, but desperate to form an alliance.

Clemmer continued, "One of the things that they asked me about was when did you get the keys and stuff like that, and I really wasn't sure when you got the keys, 'cause I wasn't there."

"Well, okay. I got the key, uh, eventually trying to be . . . I just cleared it with you, you know, our understanding that, uh, it was like five-thirty on Saturday evening."

"Oh, so you picked up the keys on Saturday?"

"Right," Rick said. "And you remember?" The conversation continued in this vein with Rick trying to superimpose a solid memory over all of Clemmer's vague recollections.

"I wish you would have told somebody, you know, when you picked it up," Clemmer said.

"Picked up the vehicle?"

"Yeah. Did you talk to any of the boys at the shop?"

"Well . . ." Rick's mind stalled out as it raced in search of a reasonable explanation.

"Was anybody there when you, when you got it?" Clemmer pressed.

"Well, uh, my, my wife was the one that I dropped off."

"Your wife dropped you off?"

"No, I dropped her off."

"Oh, to pick up the vehicle?"

"Right," Rick said, gaining confidence in this new scenario.

"Oh, she picked it up?"

"She picked it up early Monday morning."

"Oh, so it didn't happen on the weekend?" Clemmer asked.

"No."

"Okay. 'Cause they're asking me, they're asking me about it . . . about you stealing it."

"Right, right. But that's bullshit," Rick insisted. "She picked it up early, fixed the vehicle early Monday morning and I got the key from you whenever it was that . . ."

"But I don't remember the key part. That was the part I didn't remember," Clemmer repeated.

Rick then tried to pin the transfer of keys on one of the workers at the service center and attempted to convince him that there were two ignition keys on the chain.

Clemmer did not make it easy for him. "The thing is kind of freaking me out, because I'm getting too involved in this deal, you know? I mean, with your, with your wife missing and everything. I don't want to get that involved."

"Well . . ."

"And I don't want them calling me on the carpet every five minutes."

Rick worked at convincing him that if they both spouted the same details, the whole situation would blow away. But Clemmer would not commit to the scenario Rick outlined. Rick changed tactics. "I am still interested in the Jeep. Do you have a feel for when that thing might be fixed up? I'm just ready to dump this minivan."

"Yeah, I'm gonna have the fuel pump in tomorrow."

Rick then asked if Clemmer would sell his Windstar van for him. Rick thought an appeal to Clemmer's avarice would seal the deal, but Clemmer continued to equivocate. "And then I got one other problem. When you came in, you know how we give everybody the book to sign in on? For the Jeep?"

"Uh huh."

"Today, after you left, the page was missing out of that deal and there's some other numbers on there that I need. On the message book in my office."

"Yeah."

"So, then, I'm wondering if it's possible that you might have picked it up by mistake and so I can get it back," Clemmer said.

"Now what, when was this and what was . . ." Rick stalled.

"The day when you came. You know, I had that message pad that I was working on there."

"Yeah."

"And on that message pad had the Jeep deal reference and then below it there was two other numbers on that pad. I kind of need that message sheet back, so I thought maybe you might of scribbled something on it and used it as a note or something."

"Oh, I'll check," Rick said.

"Would you do that for me?"

"Yeah."

"And see if I can't get that back?"

"Boy, I'm trying to, I know I wrote down something on it. I can't, uh . . ."

"Well, that's what I thought. Maybe, you know, when you were talking on the phone, and then I went outside, did that customer and I came back. I went to retrieve that number right after you left and that, that whole sheet was gone. There's three numbers there. Your number at the top with your stuff and then there was another number and the third number was a customer. And I don't have access to that other deal. So check your notes and see if you have it."

The back-and-forth about the sheet of paper continued with Rick expressing the hope that he had not thrown it out when he "purged" a bunch of papers from his pockets and placed them into a trash can at a downtown Wendy's. Rick moved the conversation to pressuring Clemmer for a commitment to a story line.

Clemmer did not budge. "Well, you see, the only thing that scares me about this whole deal is, I don't want to get caught in a lie about the key thing if something happened bad to your wife. You know what I'm trying to say?"

"Right. Sure."

"You know, 'cause I'm not involved in this thing and I am scared to death for you, my friend. And I'm certainly scared for me, 'cause I don't want to be involved in something this serious. This is serious stuff."

"Well, you're right. Yeah. It is."

"Yeah, God forbid something bad happened and they catch me in a lie about this key thing and, shit, I don't want to go to jail over this."

"I don't want you to go to jail over this either."

"Not like over a key."

Rick continued to manipulate the story line and to try to embed his version in Clemmer's head. "It would get you in trouble if we didn't have the same recollection of what took place."

"Yeah."

"So, what are you comfortable with or what will you say?" Rick asked.

"I don't know. I guess I just better think about it, hunh?"

"Well, geez," Rick whined, "if we could kind of square away that here and now, it would certainly make me . . ."

"Sleep better?"

"Sleep better."

"I bet you would," Clemmer said.

After losing the signal and reinitiating the call, a frustrated Rick begged off the phone with the excuse that his battery was going dead.

Just before midnight, Wedding and Palmer went digging for evidence in the bags of trash the city had picked up from the curb at 351 Arcadia Place. Wedding unearthed another pair of latex gloves and an empty package of Wyler's Authentic Italian Ices.

On December 4, a small search team with the dogs trekked through Sue's neighborhood checking out all the storm drains. At one, they found a wreath of flowers laid at the opening. It seemed too obvious. It was impossible to believe that someone stuffed Sue's body into the culvert and then marked the spot. Nonetheless, the possibility had to be explored through the whole length of the pipe.

The searchers did a reconnaissance run at John James Park on Rittiman Road. Then they took a road trip up to YMCA Camp Flaming Arrow in Hunt, Texas—a traditional residential camp located on the banks of the Guadalupe River in the Texas Hill Country. Rick and his boys had camped there with the Indian Guides.

Rick and his children remained at the Cromacks' five days. When they returned to their own home, it was at 3 in the morning. They came up the road without headlights and Rick turned off the engine and drifted into the driveway.

While in the Cromack home, Rick rarely mentioned Sue's disappearance and did not demonstrate any sadness over her absence. When Margot asked him about the Suburban found across the street from his house, Rick said that Susan had test-driven it on Monday. She must have parked it in the Wellses' garage, he said.

Margot knew this was not possible. Sue would not do business at that Texaco station, since she had served on the grand jury. In fact, she'd once referred to the owner, Richard Clemmer, as a "slimeball."

But for many of Sue's friends, the possibility that Rick was responsible for Sue's disappearance seemed impossible—that he actually killed her unthinkable. Margot was a nice, considerate woman who always tried to think the best of everyone. She could have spent the rest of her life doing just that if her life had never intersected with murder.

32

On the eleventh floor at Southwestern Bell, the normal high pressure of closing the books for November stumbled into chaos. Sue was not there to lead the effort with her usual competence. The reason for her absence placed a layer of distress on top of the heavy workload. At moments, it seemed the center would not hold.

With the help of Sue's supervisor, Gary Long, the staff soldiered through the process, seeking emotional numbness in the intellectual preoccupation with numbers. Throughout the week, they clung firmly to their denial—they clutched the frail belief that any moment, Sue would walk through the door. Maybe she had amnesia and was wandering around lost. Maybe there was an urgent, plausible reason for her to leave without telling anyone. They did not allow themselves to consider that all would not be well in the end.

Somehow, they made the reporting deadline. Then their focus shifted to Sue's disappearance. Many hours of work time were consumed by employees' volunteer efforts. They walked through Sue's neighborhood putting up fliers on telephone poles, shop windows, anything that did not move.

Management worked with the Heidi Search Center to coordinate groups of staff to augment search teams. After three weeks, even those in the deepest abyss of denial rose to the surface and accepted that there would not be a happy ending.

Gary Long's holidays jarred in his head like a symphony orchestra with all the instruments tuned to a different key.

One day he was searching a basin for Sue's body or evidence of foul play. The next he was in his car with his family singing Christmas carols as he careened down the road to visit relatives in Colorado and Utah. The celebrations wound around him and he did his best to join in the spirit of the festivities. But all the while, Sue sat perched on the edge of his smile. Out of state, he could not turn to the news for an update. He grew anxious not knowing if there were new developments—if Sue of the sunny smile and boisterous laugh had been found.

Austin Hardeman was a close friend of William. His mother, Karen, was the same age as Sue and also had blonde hair and similar mannerisms. This resemblance gave William a high level of comfort in the Hardeman home. Sometimes, he called her "Mom" and he often spent the night there.

One morning after his mother's disappearance, he found Karen outside weeding around a rose bush. "I gave my mom some rose bushes once and she really liked them," he said.

"I like roses, too."

"You're just so much like my mom, if something happens, will you adopt me?"

"Oh, William. Don't worry. We'll find your mother. Everything will be all right."

Realtor Deborah Meyers received another call from the same number. This time she answered the phone. It was Rick McFarland and he wanted to know what time and what day the two of them had talked.

"I've been asked not to discuss it with anyone," she told him.

"Why not?" he asked.

"I have been advised not to discuss any details with anyone," she repeated.

"That is ridiculous," he sputtered.

Clemmer called Rick back mid-day on December 4. Rick had yet another spin on the key situation. In this scenario,

Rick arrived on the Saturday before Thanksgiving and there were two sets of keys on the chain when he took the Suburban for a test drive. At that time, with the knowledge of the person working that day, he took one set to give to his wife. "So," he concluded, "you're right. You didn't give me the key."

"Okay. Okay," Clemmer said.

"I noticed the other key already in the car and that's the one I gave to my wife."

"Okay. Okay. Well, that makes sense." Then Clemmer told Rick that Sergeant Wedding wanted to talk to him about some new evidence they found. "He said something about, 'It's more than a missing person case now.' "

"It's more of a what?" Rick asked.

"More *than* a missing person case. I don't know what that meant."

"Well, you know, the husband's always the guilty one until they find another person. So, I mean, you know, I don't know. I just don't know anymore."

"Yeah?"

"Really," Rick said.

"I bet you're freaking out."

"Oh, yeah," Rick affirmed.

Clemmer once again addressed his discomfort in lying about the key to law enforcement. "I would be just as guilty as if I participated in the crime."

"So, don't say anything about the key," Rick said. "I don't want— I mean, I'm not asking you to cooperate with me. I just wanted to, you know, touch base, like you would. It's just to make sure what details you might recall."

Poor phone reception cut their call short, and they agreed to meet in ten or fifteen minutes—but not at the Texaco station. Rick was worried the station was watched and set the rendezvous for the Big Lots store up the street.

All that day, officers from the Texas Department of Public Safety attempted to maintain mobile surveillance of Rick. They hoped he would lead them to Susan McFarland.

But Rick was either aware of the presence or just flat-out

paranoid. He made sudden turns. He never took the shortest route to any destination. He meandered all over town.

If officers were going to ensure that they could track him despite his evasive moves, they needed help. Sergeant Palmer applied to the courts for permission to install a tracking device on Rick's van.

Steven Rogers, owner of Alamo Mini Storage, had met Rick three years ago through their sons' participation in the Fox Tribe of the YMCA Indian Guides. On December 5, he got a page from Rick. He returned the call and said, "Rick, I read in the paper that the police searched your house."

"That was a courtesy search. Now there is going to be an actual search warrant. I want to store some financial records and computer stuff. It has nothing to do with the investigation, but I don't want police to see it."

Steven agreed to meet Rick at Alamo storage later that afternoon. After the call, Steven had second thoughts. He really did not want Rick storing anything at his facility.

He called back. "You know, Rick, storing items at a storage facility will not prevent police from eventually having access."

Rick said he'd changed his mind and hung up.

That day, Rick paid a visit to Dr. Gregory Jackson in Alamo Heights. His chief complaint was anxiety and depression. Rick said he was having an increased inability to pay attention—not unusual in someone under stress who was also diagnosed with adult ADD.

Rick reported difficulty in staying awake and in taking care of the three boys. He wanted a medicine that would give him more energy. Rick did not mention his wife during the interview, but did refer to the stress caused by police interviews and by angry family members and friends. He admitted that in response to his difficulty in coping, he self-medicated with ephedrine.

Dr. Jackson advised that he stop taking that drug at once. He urged him to limit his responsibilities and not take on any additional ones at this time. He should limit his interviews and social interactions to what was absolutely necessary and to get as much rest as possible.

The doctor recommended that Rick focus on activities that he was uniquely qualified to accomplish, like comforting his sons and managing basic finances. He encouraged him to get as much logistical support as possible to help him care for the children. He told Rick to get a follow-up visit with a psychologist or psychiatrist.

Dr. Jackson also examined the little finger on Rick's right hand where the tip of the digit was missing. He cleaned and dressed the wound. Dr. Jackson found Rick to be disturbed, tangential and struggling to stay awake. But, the doctor thought, this mental state was a typical one for Rick.

Sue's brother Pete was now in San Antonio and joined the search team as they covered an area by Austin Highway and Vandiver Road and a vacant lot off Stillwell Avenue. Pete, a retired homicide detective was at every search from this point on.

Many thought that Pete, with his experience as a homicide investigator, and intimate understanding of the law enforcement process, would be better equipped to handle the situation than the typical family member of a victim. Like anyone in his position, he bore the frustration of his sister remaining missing for an extended period of time—but Pete also carried an added burden that others could not know.

After years of investigating murder, he had an automatic checklist in his head that kept ticking off tasks that needed to be done. But law enforcement was not free to answer his probing questions while the case was still in progress. And Pete could not tell them what to do. It was not his case. He was not in control. It was an uncomfortable position for a veteran detective. He felt like a spectator stuck on the wrong side of the fence in the middle of the most important investigation of his life.

33

At 7 P.M. on December 5, Sue's sister Ann pulled up at 351 Arcadia Place with Sue's niece Kirsten Slaughter and her husband, Brandon. Sue's brother Pete arrived in another car with his son. Neighbor Charlene Schooling spoke to them from her front gate. She pulled no punches—she told them she was convinced that Rick was involved in the disappearance of Sue.

Ann did not want to accept that possibility—not yet—but Pete was in agreement with Charlene. Pete knew that no matter how angry Sue might have been at Rick, she would never abandon her children. The moment he'd heard about the Suburban across the street with the shovel and the gas can, he knew Rick had buried Sue, or burned her, or both.

Ann, Kirsten and Brandon went inside the house where the elder McFarlands were now in residence. Open Bibles competed with dirty dishes and scattered toys for space. Kirsten noted that there were more Bibles than there were people.

Pete tried to avoid seeing Rick by ducking into Charlene's house for a while. But when he came out, Rick was in the yard. Pete suppressed the urge to put his hands around Rick's neck and choke him until he confessed. Instead, he asked a few questions. Pete's anger grew with Rick's dazed answers and pretense that he did not know what was going on.

Pete wanted to break through that barrier of bewildered indifference. He said that he was glad the Texas Rangers

were on the job, because they were the best. "They're going
to get to the bottom of this."

Rick blanched. He looked as shocked and pained as if
Pete had just dropped a big boulder on his foot.

After Sue's family members left to go to the police station, Charlene approached Rick and asked about the boys.

"The boys are doing okay," Rick said.

Charlene then played the provocateur—for the purpose
of observing Rick's reaction. She expressed dismay at the
thought that anything bad had happened to Sue. She was
stunned by his emotionless and inappropriate response.

"You know, Susan never liked the white van. She's been
wanting a new car," he said. Then he added that he'd taken
Sue to test-drive one at the Texaco on Austin Highway.

Charlene repeated her concerns about Sue.

Rick said, "You know, I took the carpet all out of my van
and took it to be cleaned."

On December 6 at 7 A.M., Palmer, Wedding, Trevino and
Texas Ranger Marrie Garcia took their places for the surveillance of the McFarland house. Forty minutes later, Rick
and the three boys trailed out of the house and drove off. The
investigators followed Rick to his first stop, Woodridge Elementary School. Rick parked the car and briefed the boys on
what they should and should not talk about, and James and
William got out and went into the school. Rick then drove
over to the Howard Early Childhood Learning Center and
dropped off Timmy.

Driving up Lorenz Road, just west of Nacogdoches Road,
Rick pulled off onto the shoulder. As Rick talked on his cell
phone, Palmer approached the van. He informed Rick that
he had a search warrant for a sample of blood and a full set
of fingerprints. He cuffed Rick's hands in front and eased
him into the back of the state vehicle. Texas Ranger Garcia
got behind the wheel of McFarland's Windstar and followed
Palmer to University Hospital.

En route, Rick asked when he would get the property
back that was seized in the search. Palmer said that the time

frame was unknown just now. For a few blocks, Rick said nothing, then he pleaded for the return of the receipts in the plastic folder taken from the Suburban.

A registered nurse took Rick's blood sample. While he was occupied in the hospital, DPS officers attached a tracking device to his van.

As soon as the nurse finished with the procedure, Rick placed a call to his attorney, Mark Stevens. He handed the cell phone to Palmer.

"Do not ask Richard McFarland any questions. Richard McFarland has invoked his right to remain silent and not be questioned," Stevens told the Texas Ranger.

Palmer and Wedding escorted Rick to the security office at the hospital where they rolled two sets of fingerprints and a set of palm prints. Palmer used a digital camera to shoot the injuries on Rick's hands.

Having spent the morning with the search teams, Ann was unaware of Rick's forced visit to the hospital. While he was still there, she called and asked him to meet her and Kirsten at Denny's for lunch. She wanted to tell him that Sue's plans for divorce would be revealed in the news so that he could prepare the three boys for that revelation.

Rick said that he could not meet them because he was "out of pocket." He added, "My lawyer told me not to talk to you."

"Then just come and listen, because I have to tell you something," Ann said.

Rick agreed and joined the two women at the restaurant. He did not mention his adventure that morning, but asked, "Can they convict a person with only one drop of blood?"

"They can convict a person with *no* blood," Ann replied. She then told Rick about Sue's divorce plans, believing that he was unaware of them.

To her surprise, Rick didn't react as if it was news to him. He simply said, "Don't you think it was mean and unfair for her to do this at Christmastime?"

In the face of his wife's disappearance, his focus on the timing of the divorce was bizarre. Neither woman had any more doubt about his responsibility for whatever had happened to Susan.

Rick excused himself to go to the men's room. Feeling sick and angry at the conclusions they had now reached about Rick, Ann and Kirsten discussed the need to continue to treat him as if they thought he was blameless.

Kirsten wanted to lash out at him, but understood the need to suppress that desire. She did, however, insist that they would not pay for Rick's lunch.

Many miles from the Arcadia Place search site, on Foster Road in the eastern part of the county, a man spotted an odd bundle of fabric in a ditch. He stopped to examine it and discovered it was a bed sheet wrapped around a bloody mattress pad and four bloody pillows. The Bexar County Sheriff's Department took custody of this possible evidence and contacted the Texas Rangers. Many hours were consumed pursuing this lead—but it went nowhere.

That afternoon, Rick agreed to allow Ann and Kirsten to take the boys away from the home for a couple of days. He didn't want them exposed to the press around the house. He also didn't want the media to see the two women picking up the boys. He arranged a rendezvous at a nearby McDonald's. "In typical Rick fashion, the McDonald's he chose was a closed-down store," Ann said.

Knowing they were going to a McDonald's, the boys were ready to eat. Ann and Kirsten loaded them into the car and headed out to find another fast food place.

Ann was driving, so Kirsten had to deal with the situation when the kids started misbehaving. She went to the back seat and sent William up to the front.

Ann said, "William, I am very disappointed in your behavior. You're the oldest. I expect you to set an example for the other boys with all that is going on."

"You know, Aunt Ann, my dad told me that it's up to me whether he stays with us or spends the rest of his life in prison."

That statement brought an abrupt end to Ann's lecture.

At Wendy's on Broadway, Ann called the investigators and said, "William has been saying some strange things about what happened to his mom."

"We'll figure out the best thing to do and call you back," they told her.

Two minutes later, her cell phone rang. "Can you get the other two boys out of there?"

With Harley and Pete now in town, too, it was a simple request to accommodate. After James and Timmy were gone, Investigator Wedding arrived to talk to William.

Wedding had just two questions for the boy. First he asked, "When was the last time you saw your mommy?"

"I don't remember."

"Is there something you want to tell me about your mom's disappearance?"

William said that he and a friend went into 356 Arcadia Place. They saw blood inside that house that smelled weird, and he saw one of his mom's diamond earrings and one of her shoes. William rambled on for a few minutes, not saying anything that made much sense. Then he said, "My dad got down on his hands and knees and looked all over for evidence and blood." After that, William said, "I don't want to talk anymore. I want to leave."

As she left the restaurant, Ann turned to Wedding. "William said if he told me what he knows, he could send his dad to jail."

That statement shook Wedding. What did that poor young boy see? What secrets was he keeping for his father?

That night, officers searched 356 Arcadia Place. They found no blood, no earring, no evidence of a crime.

34

Carol Finley, Timmy's teacher at Howard Early Childhood Learning Center called Rick and offered to help in any way she could. Since she had a master's degree in counseling, she was willing to talk to Timmy—he could even spend the night with her if that would help.

"How can I explain what's going on with the boys?" Rick asked. "Would it be easier for a child to find out their parent was hit by a car? Or for them to think the parent was not here, but would come back?"

"Be honest with the boys," Carol urged, "and tell them the truth."

Rick then told Carol that he was a suspect in the disappearance of his wife.

Jennifer Bily phoned the McFarland home and spoke to Mona. "Is there anything I can do to help you with the boys?"

"Yes. You can help with the meals," Mona said.

Jennifer prepared and delivered dinner to the family twice a week after that call. She did not stop until Mona called and asked her to stop. "Rick doesn't want anyone coming around the house anymore," she said.

Fifty-two friends and family members—many clutching walking sticks—gathered for a detailed search of John James Park with the help of dogs and a mule. Sue's brother Pete told the gathered media, "We are grasping. At this point, it is necessary to grasp."

A great many of the volunteers were SBC employees. Also present were the brothers, cousins, and a sister-in-law of Carmen Alcaraz, who had been reported missing a month before Susan's disappearance and still had not been found. Organizing a search for Carmen was far more difficult than planning one for Sue. Carmen was last seen leaving a bar with a stranger. Where do you begin to search when you don't know where she went or who was with her?

The Alcaraz family wanted to help the Smiths find Sue, but also hoped that while searching for her, they might find Carmen. They were present every day, but their search would continue for more than a year.

On December 12, Judge Sharon McCrae of the 290th District Court authorized another search of 351 Arcadia Place. The next morning at 8, officers arrived to execute the warrant.

Texas Ranger Sergeant Shawn Palmer went to the side door and told Dick McFarland that he needed to speak to his son. The elder McFarland left to find him. When Dick did not return after a few minutes, Palmer stepped inside the house. On the first floor, he saw both of Rick's parents and his youngest son. Timmy was impressed with the regulation Stetson hat that the Texas Ranger wore—he later told his classmates that cowboys came to his house.

Palmer followed the sound of Rick's voice up to the second floor, where the door to the office was ajar. Palmer crossed the threshold and saw Rick talking on his cell phone.

After Rick ended his call, Palmer informed him of the new search warrant. He held out his hand and asked for the cell phone—Palmer knew the device also served as Rick's PDA and therefore contained possible evidence. Rick pulled the phone away to the other side of his body, forcing Palmer to grab his hand and take the device by force.

Downstairs, Palmer explained to Rick and his parents that the day's search included the use of chemicals. The house would have to air out for twenty-four hours after application. The family had to gather what they would need for that period of time and vacate the premises.

As the McFarlands prepared to leave, Palmer noticed that Rick was carrying a briefcase. He searched it and confiscated three computer disks, a packet of receipts and other documents of possible evidentiary interest.

When the family left, officers covered drawn shades in the master bedroom and Rick's office with opaque black plastic. They applied a double thickness to the skylight in the master bathroom.

When the techs arrived from Austin, they applied luminol in the master bath—on the shower surround, the commode, the vanity area, closet and doors. A bottle of cleansing gel in the shower caddy glowed bright. Several spots of luminescence winked on a small wicker wastebasket. A pattern of 90-degree droplets stood out on the bathroom scale. They applied luminol in the master bedroom and in the second-floor hall bathroom, too.

While evidence professionals were busy with spraying and photographing, other officers focused search efforts on the Windstar and its contents and Rick's home office and his computers. They confiscated seven desktop computers—five Hewlett-Packard Pavilions, one Compaq Presario, and one ePower—as well as laptops and a Qualcomm cellular phone.

In Rick's second-floor office, Palmer opened the bottom drawer of the file cabinet closest to the door and removed a box containing forty-nine rounds of Federal .380 ammunition along with three magazines for it. From a locked back room in the garage, Palmer recovered a Mossberg 12-gauge pump shotgun and a Johnson Arms .44-caliber rifle. Both weapons had dirt in their barrels and appeared unused. At 4:20, the search was complete. Palmer called Rick and left behind a printed information sheet regarding the safety hazards of the chemical spraying.

From there, the investigators headed to the Public Storage facility on Broadway to search Rick's rented unit. They recovered a Visa card in Susan's name as well as documents relating to real estate owned by the couple in Bexar and Comal Counties.

A reconnaissance team from the search center checked out the property at 119 Peck Avenue. The area consisted of several overgrown lots—none big enough to build a home. It was impossible to figure out which one was owned by Rick or why he would even want the property at all. They did not get out and search the area because of the large number of aggressive-looking dogs that were running loose.

On December 16, the ongoing search for Susan McFarland stepped up a notch. At the request of Sue's sister Ann, Texas EquuSearch, a Houston-based mounted search and recovery organization joined in the hunt.

Before beginning for the day, Tim Miller, director of the group, stopped by 351 Arcadia and asked Rick to help them search. Rick requested and received a business card from Miller, but never called and did not participate.

With dogs, horses, helicopters, all-terrain vehicles, a high-tech ground penetrating system and fifty local volunteers, Texas EquuSearch explored a number of areas including Olmos Basin Park in China Grove, open land near Salado Creek and an oil field near Loop 410—one of the two circular highways that wrapped around San Antonio.

Before the searchers set out on their mission, Tim Miller said, "If there is any ground at all that looks like it's been disturbed, call in on it." The equipment the team brought to San Antonio had the capability of scanning up to eight feet deep. The shovel found in the back of the Suburban made the possibility of a burial likely.

In Mahncke Park, they checked out the source of a foul odor with dogs from the Greater Bexar Search and Rescue Team. The remains found were not human, but a squad of firefighters searched the whole length of the tunnel for everyone's peace of mind.

At the end of the day, the only suspicious items uncovered were a bone and a sweater. Palmer turned these items over to Sergeant Wedding, but said they appeared to have been outside far too long to be connected with Sue's disappearance.

Carrie Miller was one of the many who helped out with the searches. She did the best she could, but was not confident that she would know what was important when she saw it.

When she was told to watch out for snakes, she wanted to leave. But she stuck it out for Sue. No matter how hard she tried to banish the worry from her mind, snakes wriggled through her thoughts with every step she took.

Harriet Wells expected to see masses of media vehicles on Arcadia when she visited her old house. But she was shaken when she pulled into the street of her new place and saw satellite uplink trucks, vans, cars with cardboard press signs pressed in the windows. She worried: Was another woman missing?

Unbeknownst to Harriet, another chapter in the disappearance of Sue McFarland had just begun on her street. A few doors down from her home, the search headquarters set up in St. David's Episcopal Church, and the media followed like puppies to a bag of biscuits.

The next day, Texas EquuSearch went back to work. "We're looking for old, lonely roads. Roads going into fields—anything like that, where it's easy access and easy to dump something," Miller told the gathered crowd of volunteers and media.

About eighty volunteers were on hand on this day—searching through woods and fields for freshly dug earth, bones, clothing or strong odors. They searched Brackenridge Park near the H-E-B Science Treehouse—an area where Rick had been seen. Cadaver dogs were sent to examine a hill near the Witte Museum. They found a bounty of used tires and old cans, but uncovered nothing connected to Susan McFarland.

Once again, Rick did not assist with the search, but he was paying attention to it. About noon that day, he drove to Alamo Stadium and parked in the lot for one hour. From that vantage point, he could spy on the volunteer searchers as they worked in Brackenridge Park.

• • •

While Rick made his observations, David took a couple of the boys to Wendy's. There, Julie Speer approached him to encourage counseling for the children.

The next day, Julie received a call from Rick. She asked him how he was doing.

"Bad. I'm having to practice creative thinking," Rick said. He then asked Julie about the conversation she had with his brother David. Julie told Rick where he could get counseling for his boys.

"I've been put in a box by legal counsel because of the peculiarities of this," Rick said. "I cannot take a breath without going to them."

"I think the boys might need help dealing with this," Julie urged.

"I hadn't thought about that, but my brother is in town and he's good at slapping me around. But the boys are fine—what I need help with is after-school care."

On December 20, a Heidi Search Center reconnaissance team checked out a creek by East Houston Street near the interchange of Loop 410 and Interstate Highway 10. The Indian Guides had an outing in that area in the past, but the search scouts found nothing suspicious there.

Next-door neighbor Charlene Schooling always had a clear view from her home of the primary color scheme of the airy, open McFarland kitchen. The week before Christmas, that changed. Rick covered all the windows with placemats.

Charlene could still see the yard next door, and it broke her heart. Sue was particular about the upkeep of her property. Now depressing mounds of brown leaves were strewn everywhere.

Charlene had to do something—for Sue's sake. She knocked on the front door to ask if she could mow up the leaves. Rick's brother David answered the door and stepped out on the porch to talk. "Anything you want to do to brighten things up around here is just great," David said.

Charlene asked about the boys, about Rick and about his parents. David said, "All is as well as can be expected." He repeated many times how hard the situation was on everyone. But he did not mention Sue's name even once.

"Did you like Susan?" Charlene asked.

"Well, that's a kind of hard question to answer."

"Why?"

"Well, we went to the same high school, but ran with different crowds."

Charlene did not quite understand that evasive answer. But beneath its surface, she saw clear signs that the McFarland family's attitude toward Sue was not an adoring one.

"I just hope they find Susan soon—whether she's dead or alive," David continued. "And if my brother is guilty of what it seems they all are expecting, then I wish they'd just get this thing over with so everyone can have some closure. It's so depressing around here. I can't wait to go home," David said.

Late one night, a neighbor in a home with a glass-covered back overlooking the McFarland house was up late. The rest of her family was tucked in bed, asleep. She laid out clothing for the kids to wear to school the next day, then went through the house turning out all the lights. When her home was as dark as the outdoors, she paused by a window and surveyed the house full of questions that backed up to hers.

She saw the back door open and shrunk back into the shadow of darkness. Rick stepped out onto the porch. She did not think he could see her with all the lights out in her home. But Rick walked to the driveway, bent down as if he were picking up a small rock. He pulled back his arm and hurled it in her direction. She held her breath waiting for the sound of crashing glass. Nothing.

Rick bent down again and repeated his actions. Still she heard not a sound. She did not know if he really threw a rock at her house or if he was just faking it. She did know, however, that he was trying to intimidate or frighten her—and he succeeded. She imagined he was concerned that she might have seen something on the night of November 25 and wanted her to be too scared to say a word.

She was frightened. But she was also angry—angry at the pain he'd caused his three boys, angrier still at the impact his actions had on her 6-year-old daughter. Her little girl was fearless before this past Thanksgiving. Now, she was a timid, terrified rabbit. She would not set foot outside alone. She wouldn't even go upstairs unless one of her parents accompanied her.

In William's Sunday school class at First Presbyterian Church, Melissa St. John gave him a piece of ceramics—a white dove Christmas ornament—that he had made as a class art project before his mother's disappearance. All he wanted to do now was destroy it.

Melissa told him it was not a good idea to make an irreversible decision while there was so much chaos in his life. She encouraged him not to do anything until his world was back to normal. After the contemporary church service, William rushed up to Melissa and threw his arms around her. Melissa's heart swelled—William was usually averse to touching.

That display of affection had an impact on Rick McFarland as well. After observing it, he approached church personnel and insisted that they prohibit anyone from talking to his children about their mother.

In his class at the church, James McFarland asked his teacher, "Does God send people to heaven who have killed?"

35

It seemed as if everyone was worried about the boys. What did they know? What did they fear? How were they coping? Terrell Hills police fielded a constant stream of calls about the children's well-being. Police wanted Child Protective Services to move in and take action. They filed paperwork requesting CPS look into the situation. Individual caseworkers were concerned, but getting the lumbering, overloaded bureaucracy into motion was a challenge.

Detectives kept a close eye on the boys, though. They had serious concerns that Rick would grab them and run. They received vague information about overheard bits of conversation indicating that Rick planned to flee to Mexico with his kids. The border was only a couple of hours away. Although none of the rumors could be verified, the possibility remained real, their investigators' vigilance constant.

Margot Cromack was determined to make the boys' Christmas as normal as possible. She baked Christmas cookies with them and took them on holiday outings.

The thought of taking the children out of the chaos of their home and relocating them in St. Louis was considered and rejected. The prevailing opinion was that maintaining the regular routine as closely as possible was the best plan.

No one wanted to speculate on the long-term effect this event would have on the rest of their lives. But Rick McFarland declined all offers of counseling for his boys.

• • •

On December 20, the last day of school before Christmas break, Sergeant Palmer went to Woodridge Elementary School. First, he talked to a reluctant James. "I wish my mother would be here for Christmas," he said.

"I am working very hard to find your mother, but I need some help," Palmer said. "Do you know where she is?"

"Mom said she was going to Amarillo without us."

To Palmer's ears, this line sounded coached and memorized.

Then James asked, "Do you think my mom is dead?"

"I don't know. But I am working very hard to find her."

James talked about a car with blood in it and then said, "Some people have gardens and they could cut themselves in the garden. Can I go back to class?"

William entered the room ignoring the presence of the Ranger. He sat down and rolled his eyes. "I will not talk to the police," he said.

"We can talk about whatever you want," Palmer coaxed.

"I don't want to talk about anything."

"I am working hard to find your mom," Palmer said. "Do you know any clues that would help?"

William's conversation wandered through details about his spy kit and his microscope, the house across the street and an apartment in St. Louis where DNA was found. He was talking in a normal tone of voice, but anger flared hot in his eyes.

"William, what do you think I should do to find your mom?"

"Give everyone in the world a lie detector test."

"Who should I start with?"

"My dad."

"What should I ask him?"

" 'Did you do it?' "

"Do what?"

"Ask my mom to leave. My mom and dad were arguing and stuff." After that detail slipped through his lips, William changed subjects, castigating Palmer for destroying his

GameCube with that powder—the luminol. Then he asked to go back to class.

Kim Gueldner's third grade class at Woodridge Elementary shook with the trauma of Sue's disappearance. They worried about their classmate James—it had been nearly a month and the whereabouts of his mother were still a mystery. Many worried that their mothers would be next.

But Sue was more than just a fellow student's mom—she was their Junior Achievement teacher, too. She came to see them once a week and taught them about towns and cities. She helped them put together a newspaper, build model homes out of cardboard and create an accurate blueprint of their classroom.

They missed her smile, her vivacity, her words of praise. They needed to do something—anything—to express their grief and fear. Kim had an idea. The class would submit Sue's name as a candidate for the Junior Achievement Volunteer of the Year award.

Each of the children wrote a letter to Mrs. McFarland. These notes were submitted with the application. The words of the children were poignant and heart-rending.

Thank you for being such a good mother and a teacher. I wish you could come back but you are not here. Please come back. I will tell God if he could tell me where are you. My and your Christmas present will be you to come back.

James is worried about you. I hope you are ok. I miss you so much. My mom misses you so much. The hole class misses you. Well, I hope your ok.

We'll never forget you. You are a good friend to us. A lot of people are scard. We all wish you wher still here. I hope we find you. Your like $2,556,000 to me. I think your botuful. If you enterd a bouty contest you would come in first place.

I hope we find you because you are so fun and wonderful. Sorry we were so loud.

I wish this has never happen. You missed Thanksgiving. I hope you don't miss Christmas.

Later that day, Rick was at the school for the annual Holiday Happening. Principal Linda Schlather and another administrator escorted him to the classrooms. They tried to be subtle, but Rick recognized the special treatment and asked them about it.

"It's as much for your own protection as anything else," Linda explained.

"What do you mean?"

"There are people here who are convinced you committed this crime. We want to prevent them from saying anything to you," Linda said. But that was only part of the story. She was also motivated to keep him in her sight because of the responsibility she felt for the safety of the school and everyone in it.

In honor of Sue McFarland, Charlene and her daughter Susan picked up enough poinsettias for the front porch of every house on their block. They wrapped the pots in blue paper—Sue's favorite color—and silver bows. They attached a card that read:

Remember Susan McFarland.
P.U.S.H.
Pray Until Something Happens.

On December 23, probate court conducted a hearing about the estate of Susan McFarland. Sue's family had filed papers to ensure that the estate was used for the care of the boys. They were concerned that since Rick had no income of his own, Sue's money would be spent to pay his legal expenses instead of being used for the boys' welfare. Although Sue's paychecks from Southwestern Bell continued to be direct-deposited in the McFarlands' joint account, Rick was not paying the mortgage.

The court ruled that Rick would maintain control of Sue's salary. They did, however, appoint George Dowlen, a former judge, as receiver of Sue's assets and inheritance from her mother. He was authorized to use those funds for the education, support and medical needs of the three boys.

In Missouri, anxiety trampled on any vestiges of Christmas spirit. Emails and phone calls kept the edgy family connected in distress rather than celebration. On the Internet, they checked San Antonio websites as obsessively as if they were driven by intense religious fervor.

No one slept well. Everyone's productivity plummeted as their minds were distracted by thoughts of Sue.

Sally the dog was in the McFarlands' front yard when Susan Schooling gave her a bone on Christmas Day. She then went up to the McFarland house with two presents for each of the boys. Mona invited her in. Timmy rushed up to her and tugged on her shirt. "Susan, Susan. Guess what? My mommy is lost. Did you know my mommy was lost?"

As Timmy spoke, Susan's heart shattered like a fragile glass ball knocked from a Christmas tree. Rick wanted to talk to Susan privately. She cringed—she did not want to talk to him at all. She knew he was guilty of harming Sue. In fact, she felt as if her presence in that home was a betrayal of Sue. But she wanted to be there for the boys.

Rick asked if she could take care of the boys for a couple of hours after school and make dinner for them. Susan's first inclination was to agree for the sake of William, James and Timmy. She gave Rick a non-committal response.

When Susan did not return right away, her mother, Charlene, was concerned and went over to bring her home. Rick answered the door and invited her inside. Charlene's head spun as she encountered reminders of Sue everywhere. But she was even more disturbed at the things that were not the same. The house was a mess. The Christmas tree was not in its usual place and it stood as straight as the Leaning Tower of Pisa—the ornaments hanging drunkenly from its branches.

After the Schoolings left, Rick called Dee Ann Dowlen. "How's Christmas going?" she asked.

"It's funky," he said. "I imagine I'll be calling more since George is the receiver for the estate."

"Do you want to talk to George?"

"No. But the boys want to talk to you."

One by one, the three children took the phone and thanked Dee Ann for the Christmas presents she and George sent to them.

That evening, Rick, his parents and his sons had Christmas dinner at the Cromack home.

The day after Christmas, Rick and the boys went over to the Schooling home to offer thanks for their presents. As Charlene opened the door, William was looking at Rick and screaming, "I hate you!"

The photograph of Sue featured on her MISSING posters hung on the Schooling refrigerator. Charlene rushed over to take it down, concerned that it would upset the boys. Rick blocked her way—he stood in front of it staring at the picture as if he had never seen it before.

When the boys came into the home, Timmy was his usual self—all over the house chasing and romping with the Schoolings' dogs. James and William, however, were unusually quiet. William brought the i-Zone camera he'd received from the Schoolings so that he could use it to take their picture. As Charlene posed for the shot, her throat clutched tight—she thought William was looking more and more like Susan with every passing day.

36

The McFarland boys attended riding camp over the Christmas break. Margot arrived each morning to take them to the ranch. One brisk morning, the boys emerged from the house in lightweight clothing unsuitable for the chill in the air. Margot detoured past her home and grabbed sweatpants and sweatshirts to keep them warm.

At noon, Margot always drove back to the ranch to pick them up and return them to their home and their grandparents. One day when she arrived, Rick was there. He was walking around the collection of old cars by the stable with James. If Rick kicked the wheel of car. James kicked the wheel. If Rick peered in a window, James did, too. When Rick put his hands in his pockets, James likewise stuck his down deep.

A comment Sue made nearly two years earlier drifted up into Margot's mind. "If I divorced Rick right now, James would never speak to me again."

Margot pooh-poohed that idea at the time. But, now, watching James echoing Rick's every move, she saw the strong connection between father and son and knew that Sue had grounds for her concern.

A case like the disappearance of Susan McFarland generated a lot of irrelevant leads. One of the oddest of all was a phone call on December 26 from a woman who'd spoken to a psychic in the interior of Mexico. Susan McFarland was alive and being held captive by cocaine-snorting thugs in an old abandoned house, the psychic said. These thugs were in regular cell phone contact with Richard McFarland.

Other tips had a stronger connection to reality and required the time of investigators to follow them up. Employees at Ruben Auto Center in Seguin—forty miles east of San Antonio—discovered a burned human body in the back of a pickup truck on New Year's Day. From the beginning, investigators thought it unlikely that it was Susan McFarland. They went out to the scene just the same. The trip was fruitless. Susan McFarland was still missing.

The neighbor with the window overlooking the McFarland house returned home after being away for the holidays. Once again, she was up later than the rest of the family and walked room to room turning out the lights. Once again, she paused by a window and looked over there.

As if on cue, Rick came out of his house and stopped at the same spot as before. This time, he did not re-enact the rock-throwing. Instead, he threw his arm up and swung it around in a broad motion as if to say, "Come on over."

She staggered back from the window. As frightened as she was, she did not want Rick to know of her fear. She stayed away from him as much as possible, but sometimes contact was unavoidable. When she did see him at school or in the street, she donned a façade of polite normalcy. She did not want McFarland mad at her. She did not know what he would do.

On January 2, Susan Schooling went on line to do research on after-death communications. She was ready to try any means to locate Sue McFarland. She was desperate to do something—anything—to find answers to the mystery that shredded the peace of the neighborhood and the hearts of three young boys.

She sent emails to three or four websites that appeared credible. One hour later, she received a call from Scotland. It was psychic Christine Toomey. She said she could not fight the urge to call. She felt an extreme, powerful energy—Sue McFarland was trying hard to communicate.

Christine was certain that Sue's body was burned—all police would find were charred bones. She said that finances were a major struggle between her and her killer, and a generous amount of money was involved.

The psychic claimed that Sue said she was okay now and in a better place. She was with an elderly woman—a small, frail older woman—possibly her mother.

Christine also delivered a warning from Sue to Susan: "Absolutely do not go over to the house when you would be alone with Rick." Sue does not want you there, the psychic said. She wants you to stay away.

About the manner of Sue's death, Christine said she died from a blow to the head. "It was real quick and fast. She did not feel it." It was going to take a long time, however, to resolve the case. It would probably be a year before Rick went to jail.

"They found already, or will find, a red sweater or red top in or nearby a creek, lake or ravine, with other debris that belongs to Susan. That is what she was wearing when she was murdered. He left her clothed when he burned her body, and that item was blown away by the wind, while burning, into a nearby area like a creek bed. They will find it."

Finally, Susan asked where Sue's body was located. Christine was vague, but said that Sue kept telling her it was twenty-five minutes or twenty-five miles from where Rick was located. When investigators found Sue's body, it was 15.2 miles from 351 Arcadia Place—a twenty-five-minute drive.

On January 3, Sergeant Palmer called Margot Cromack on her cell phone and left a message when he got no answer. At 5:50 P.M., surveillance reported that Rick arrived at the Cromack house. Five minutes later, Margot returned Palmer's call.

The background noises prompted Palmer to believe she was either outside or in a car. He asked her if she was alone. She assured him that she was. As he continued his conversation, Palmer sent Sergeant Wedding over to drive by the

Cromack home. In a couple of minutes, Wedding was there. He spotted Margot on the porch near her front door. Standing close to her—leaning in and listening to the conversation—was Rick McFarland.

Wedding relayed the information to Palmer. Interesting, Palmer thought.

Rick continued to bug Susan Schooling about caring for his boys after school. "I have to get a job. I have to bring some income in now that she's gone."

Susan said she would think about it, hoping he would drop it. But he didn't. After giving it more thought, she knew she could not bear to spend every day in the house where Sue died. She could not tolerate being around the man who killed her. She loathed the idea of being paid by him. The thought sickened her. She told Rick that she could not do it because it conflicted with her class schedule.

Rick, as usual, did not take no for an answer. And Susan's distress escalated. Her father Mike intervened, writing a note to Rick that read, "I don't think it would be a good idea under the circumstances. I think you should get someone else." He dropped the note in the McFarland mailbox.

Rick came out right away, read it quickly and chased after Mike Schooling. Rick followed Mike into the house and confronted Susan. "My mom is gone now. And I thought you'd take care of them. I am so pissed. Now what am I going to do?"

Susan, Charlene and Mike cited the class scheduling problem again and again. Rick kept blaming them for his problems. Then he blurted out: "Now that I've been named the prime suspect, are you thinking I'm going to get a chain saw and chop you all up?"

The Schoolings had no response for that outburst. But it sure gave them something to ponder.

Sue's family called a hiatus in the search efforts before Christmas. They wanted the staff and volunteers to have some normalcy in their holiday season. On January 5, the search geared up again. Searchers revisited Brackenridge Park and combed an area near the Sunken Gardens and Alpine Trail.

Early in the evening of January 6, Sergeants Palmer and Wedding met with Margot Cromack at the Terrell Hills Police Department. They questioned her about her relationship to Rick. Palmer then asked her about providing information to McFarland and allowing him to listen in on the phone conversation she had with him.

Margot denied ever allowing Rick to eavesdrop on a telephone call. She insisted she was not at home when she talked to Palmer three days earlier. Wedding and Palmer knew that was not true.

Margot volunteered that the only reason she maintained contact with Rick was that she wanted to keep an eye on the three boys. That was all she cared about, she said.

Palmer called Sue's sister Ann. "I want you to be very careful around Margot Cromack."

"What do you mean?" she asked.

"She has led me down rabbit trails."

"What are rabbit trails?"

"Places that lead us nowhere," he said. "She's been sharing information inappropriately with Rick. I don't think you can trust her."

"What am I supposed to do with this information?" Ann asked.

"Tell your family members and Sue's close friends."

Two years after the fact, Margot continued to insist the officers were mistaken.

On January 7, law enforcement followed Rick and his son Timmy to The Spy Store. There Rick asked about bug detectors that could identify listening devices and telephones. He wanted to know if they worked on cell phones, too. He left without making a purchase.

While Rick was running around with his youngest son, William and James were at the Miller home. Carrie noticed that William had adopted a caretaker role. In response to

James, he often made parental remarks like "James, do not do that," or "Very good, James." His caring warmed her heart, but the reason he assumed this role was as chilling as a Dean Koontz plot.

In the middle of that day, Stephanie, in a fit of anger, let the F bomb fly. After her mother had chastised her, William gave Carrie advice on how to correct her children when they got in trouble. He demonstrated how his father laid them across the bed and used one or both arms to spank them with a small board. "One time, I had to tell my teacher I could not sit down because my bottom hurt too much."

Later that day, Carrie walked into Wesley's room where William was playing Nintendo. When he turned toward Carrie, his eyes were moist and heavy with threatened tears. "What's wrong, William?" she asked.

"I miss my mom."

"Where do you think she is?"

"She's out looking for a new husband."

"Oh, c'mon, William. Do you really think your mom would go off and leave you and James and Timmy to look for a new husband and not be here for Thanksgiving?"

"Yes. She needed a little break from us. She'll be back."

Carrie now knew what Rick had been telling the boys about their mother. It sickened and enraged her.

When she left the room, Wesley said, "William, do you think your dad did something to her?"

"No," William said. "Some people do, but I don't."

37

The next day, the boys came over to Carrie's house with a box of books. "We're selling them," William said. "Mom was the only one in the house who made money and now she's gone and we need some."

Carrie looked through the box and spotted *Love You Forever*—a book about a mother's love for her child. "William, don't you want to keep this one?"

"I'm too old for it," William said.

Instinctively, Carrie knew that this line had been scripted, too.

A couple of hours later, Carrie needed to run errands and told the McFarland boys they needed to go home.

"I don't want to go home," William said. "Can I go with you?"

"I can't take you anywhere without your dad's permission."

A call to the McFarland home went unanswered. "Maybe the police took him," James suggested.

While the boys peddled their books, Rick had his own quick cash scheme going. He went up to Glass works on New Braunfels Avenue at the Sunset Ridge Center in Alamo Heights. He purchased a selection of art glass, went home with his purchases and listed them on eBay. If he was able to get a bid that exceeded the price he paid, he sold it. If not, he carted it up and returned it to the store. After several visits, the shopkeepers figured out that something strange was

going on. But before they could assemble all the pieces of
the puzzle, Rick's shopping trips to their store ended.

Fox Broadcasting sent a team to San Antonio to pursue the
Susan McFarland disappearance for their newsmagazine
show, *The Pulse*. They wanted to interview Harriet Wells
from her home across the street from the McFarlands'. But
the house that Ned's parents built in 1938 was demolished
by the new property owner and new construction was under
way. The news team taped her on the lot where her house
used to be.

Along with Catherine Herridge, the cameramen crossed
the street and invaded the Schooling home—interviewing
Charlene at great length. That afternoon, a short while after
the team left, Charlene was at her front door saying goodbye
to a friend. She heard the distinct sound of a shave-and-
a-haircut knock on the back door. She was certain it was
Rick and ducked into her half-bath to avoid him.

She waited and waited for him to give up and leave. He
knocked and knocked. Finally, all was quiet. Charlene
emerged thinking the coast was clear. That was what Rick
wanted her to think. He was still by the door in a ball cap, a
black t-shirt and black jeans—he had cracked the door open
and his hand rested on the inside of the door.

"Hey, Rick," she said. "What can I do for you?"

"I want to talk with you. I'm really angry."

"Do you want to come in?"

He stepped inside the kitchen door. Charlene walked to
the dining room table and sat down, hoping he would follow
her lead. Instead, he stood in the area between the kitchen
and dining room, pacing. Back and forth. From side to side.
He swiveled on the ball of his foot to make each turn.

Charlene was shaking. She was scared. His pacing only
magnified her anxiety. But she wanted Rick to think she was
at ease and threw her legs up on the table as if in casual
abandon—two friends talking, nothing more.

Still Rick paced and ranted. "I just don't understand you,

Charlene. Do you just get off on talking to all those TV people who are in and out of here every day?"

Charlene looked at him and looked at the chair at the table. At last, Rick got the message and slid down beside her.

"Rick, do you think I enjoy seeing myself on TV without my hair done and no makeup on?"

"So, why do you talk to them?"

"They catch me every time I step outside my door."

"Why don't you just tell them 'No comment'?"

"Because we need to find Susan, Rick."

"I thought you loved my boys. I thought you cared about them. Here I am trying to protect them from publicity and you are encouraging it."

"Rick, I do it because we need to find Susan. The boys need their mother," Charlene pleaded.

Rick just shrugged.

Charlene wanted to scream at him—wanted to demand that he tell her what he did to Susan, where he left her body. But she kept her peace.

"And another thing," Rick continued, "I understand you've been telling neighbors that I asked you to lie for me."

"That's a downright lie, Rick. I never said that to anyone."

"Well. Who was that who was here today that you were accommodating?"

"Fox. It was for *The Pulse*."

"*The Pulse?* What's that?

"It's a new show like *Dateline* or *Twenty/Twenty*."

"Charlene, I want you to call them and tell them not to air it," Rick said as he stood and walked over to her telephone. He picked up the receiver and brought it over to her.

"I'm not going to call them, Rick."

Rick pushed the phone at her.

"No, Rick. Even if I did, it wouldn't do any good. They've talked to the District Attorney and the police. These people are from New York. They are not going to do what I say."

"They're from New York?" Rick asked with widened eyes and furrowed brow.

"Yes, Rick."

"Then this is national?"

"Yes."

Rick looked as if the possibility never crossed his mind. He excused himself and walked toward the back door.

"You can use the front door, Rick."

"No, no. I want to go out the way I came in."

Charlene realized then that she did not know how he managed to get in her backyard, and walked to the door to find out. The pickets on a section of fence hung askew. Rick had pulled out the nails holding in the bottoms of the tall boards on the privacy fence and wiggled under them. Because of the angle, he could not go back through the fence the same way. He borrowed Charlene's ladder, propped it against the fence, climbed to the top and jumped down to his porch.

Now Charlene was worried about the return of the Fox team. Earlier, she had given them permission to come back at night and use their infrared cameras to shoot film of Rick inside his house from her windows.

She called and told them plans had changed a bit because of Rick's visit. "I told you that you could come and I'm not going to go back on that. But when you come, you have to park down the street, approach the house one by one and enter by the door on the side of the house opposite from the McFarlands' home."

The Fox team made their cloak-and-dagger entrance and headed up to the second floor. They caught Rick watching television and eating a bowl of ice cream. But they wanted him to stand up. Catherine Herridge asked Charlene to call him, since he'd have to stand up to answer the phone.

"Are you kidding?" Charlene asked. "After I told you about today, you want me to call him? You must be kidding."

Instead, the producer called the McFarland home. The cameraman shot the video as Rick moved across the room to pick up the phone. Mission accomplished.

38

Parents at Woodridge Elementary School were restless and on edge. Unfounded rumors and half-truths fed into the gaping maw of their fears. They were afraid that Rick would come on campus and hurt their children. They wanted him to be denied access to the school.

Principal Linda Schlather addressed the PTO to inform them about the law and reassure them about the security of the school. Rick is a parent, she told them, and as such has, by law, the right to be at the school as long as he does not violate any school policies.

"Safety is always our concern," she said. "We know who he is and we will be vigilant." She added that the desire of the faculty and the staff was that the McFarland boys have as normal a time as possible when they were in the school.

On January 11, Sergeant Wedding reviewed a stack of accumulated phone messages. One call was from Jim Tutt, who described himself as the stepson of Gil Medellin, who lived out in rural southeast Bexar County on South W.W. White Road. Tutt said his stepfather had seen a Suburban matching the description of the one police had recovered, driving up and down by his house four or five times on the night before Thanksgiving.

Around 7:30 at night, the neighbor who faced the McFarlands' backyard was home alone with her 6-year-old daughter.

Her husband was out at a gymnastics class with their two older children. The phone rang. When she answered her ears were filled with the nastiest and vilest sexual suggestions she ever heard. Her first thought was of Rick, but she was not certain. The next day at Carrie Miller's house, she listened to a previously recorded message from Rick on their voicemail. Then she knew—the obscene caller was Rick. The purity he had sworn to Promise Keepers was now dust in the wind.

Kirsten Slaughter told the *St. Louis Post-Dispatch*, "It's horrible going through this moment-by-moment, every day. It is the focus of our lives, and sometimes it's overwhelming. My daughter can't sleep. I was incapacitated during Christmas. I still have a shred of hope that Sue is alive. But probably not."

Ann Carr complained to the reporter that her family had to go through Rick's attorney to communicate with Sue's three boys. "We believe they are in a very stressed situation, and it's been made difficult for us to see them. That's been hard on all of us."

In that same January 12 article, Terrell Hills Police Chief Larry Semander was quoted as well. "We have no way of knowing specifically what happened to her, but it would appear that she didn't leave of her own accord."

Meanwhile, Rick avoided Sue's family, held police and press at arm's length and made no effort to solve the mystery of his wife's disappearance.

Rick dropped William and James off at the corner near the Miller home and drove off with Timmy in his car on the afternoon of January 12. The two boys stayed at that house for hours. At 5, the Millers needed to take Wesley to his basketball game and sent the boys home. In minutes, they were back. The door was locked, they said, and they could not get in.

Carrie tried to reach Rick by his cell phone. When that didn't work, she sent the boys up to Karen Hardeman's house. There they played on the trampoline until dark, then

moved inside and sat down at the PlayStation. Karen continued the quest for Rick. When she reached him, Rick said,
"William knows the code to get in."

"They are hungry, Rick."

"There's dinner in the refrigerator. Or it's probably still
sitting out on the porch where the church left it."

"I'll keep them here until they can be supervised at
home," Karen said.

"I'll be home by eight," Rick promised.

Karen fed the boys along with her children. They watched
TV, played some video games. Eight o'clock came and went.
At 8:40, Karen called Rick again. He told her he was at the
grocery store in the check-out line and would be home in a
few minutes.

It was a school night and not only did Karen want
William and James to get settled in for the night, she had two
children of her own to worry about. She and her husband
loaded up the car with the two McFarland boys and their son
and daughter and drove the short distance to 351 Arcadia.

Karen's family waited outside in the car while she went
inside with the boys. The house was pitch black but when
she flipped on a light switch, she was appalled at what she
saw—boxes and papers were everywhere, dirty dishes piled
on every surface. It looked as if the cops had torn it apart
while searching, and all these weeks later, Rick had put
nothing away.

On top of that, the cat was locked in the bathroom wail-
ing for freedom and food. After taking care of his cat and
bringing in the casserole from the front porch, William said,
"We'll be fine. You can go now."

"I'm not leaving you here alone. You two go upstairs and
take a bath."

"We took baths yesterday," William objected.

Karen insisted they needed another one tonight. James
went upstairs, but William stayed on the first floor trying to
get Karen out of the house.

Finally, between 9:30 and 10, Rick rambled home with

Timmy. He thanked Karen for her help, but left the impression that he thought it had been unnecessary in the extreme.

Karen told a friend the story of her experience that night. Soon, it was all over the neighborhood. Someone—and every person in the neighborhood who was asked pointed the finger at someone else—knew it was time to take action. That person called CPS to report the neglect of the boys. The caller didn't think the urgency of the situation was being appreciated by the person at the other end until she said that she thought there was a danger of a hostage situation and that the father was supposed to be on medication, but was not taking it. The caller could almost hear the red flags hoisting to the top of the pole.

When Karen heard that CPS was called in, she said, "If they find me with a knife in the back, you know who did it."

39

The next evening, Texas Ranger Palmer visited Gil Medellin. Gil confirmed what his stepson said about the Suburban and added that in the days before Thanksgiving, he also saw a black SUV on a different night. He tried to flag down the driver, who would not stop.

More ominously, Gil said that he had seen smoke rising from the area around the abandoned farmhouse during daylight hours that week. Palmer drove past the property but did not enter, because the driveway was blocked by a pile of dirt. He saw nothing suspicious.

On January 14, Child Protective Services went to the schools to interview the boys. William told the representatives that he and James got in big trouble when CPS came by the house. "We were supposed to go inside if we saw anyone from CPS, law enforcement or the media, and we didn't," he told them. "My dad says now we may have to go to an orphanage for a while."

William said that they got in trouble when they called each other names or when he and James ganged up on Timmy. If they misbehaved, he made them sit on the trampoline and "get a little pounding." That, he said, meant that they had to "body slam each other." Sometimes, he related, their dad would say, "Turkey jump fast," then grab the small hairs at their napes and pull them up.

The boy explained that there were five levels of punishment. On level one, his dad popped them with his hand. On level five, he popped them with a rod on their rumpuses. He said his dad began using the rod after reading a Bible verse that said, "Don't use the rod, spoil the child." William claimed that the last time he had marks left on his rumpus from the rod was when he ran away and called his dad curse words.

He said his mom gave them light pops, but didn't have levels of punishment. He felt safe with Mom. He did not feel safe with Dad.

James told CPS that neither he nor William had ever been hurt taking care of themselves. He expressed concern that his brothers might lie because they thought their dad was mean. But, Dad, he said, was just administering punishment.

Timmy reported that his dad pinched him and "hurt his bones." He demonstrated this punishment by squeezing both his shoulders hard. "My dad pinches my bones into crumbs." Then, he thumped his head with his finger and said his dad did that a lot, too.

That same morning at 8 A.M., Sergeant Palmer met with staff and volunteers from the Heidi Search Center. A new lead demanded a search by the San Antonio River from Mulberry Avenue down to the end of River Road.

Searchers walked with slow deliberation down both sides of the river searching for signs of anything suspicious. Palmer spotted the telltale indications of a recent burial site. He called in a request for evidence techs.

While waiting for their arrival, Palmer shot photographs of the spot. He kept everyone far enough away from the site to avoid contamination, but brought the staff close enough to learn the significance of his discovery. "See how different this spot looks from the area around it?" he said as he pointed out the visual and tactile anomalies of freshly turned earth.

Throughout the weeks of searching, Palmer—present at every location—used each occasion as a teaching opportunity. It was clear that he wanted the Heidi Search Center staff to be as knowledgeable as possible to add to their effectiveness in the future. Kate Kohl, executive director of the organization, felt that both he and Sergeant Wedding treated them with uncommon respect and inclusion. "They really brought us into the circle of trust," she said.

When the evidence team arrived, they all stood back and watched the slow, methodical process of uncovering a grave. Using techniques employed at archeological dig sites, they excavated small layers of dirt, transporting it with care to a selected site for further examination later.

As they approached the buried object, the smell of death—a nauseating blend of sweet and sour—rose from the hole and permeated the senses of the onlookers. They rocked with a violent personal revulsion at the assault. At the bottom of the grave, there was a body—the carcass of a dog.

Kate—no stranger to dead animals, having encountered many during flood searches—was surprised by the difference and intensity of the stench. The smell that emanated from the grave was far more raw and primal than the odor of decay she encountered out in the open.

Moments after the techs realized there were no human remains at this site, Shawn Palmer left the search area, urgency electrifying his every move. Kate noticed the change in his demeanor as he hurried off to his car. She wondered about its cause, but did not suspect what the afternoon would reveal.

Palmer caught up with Sergeant Wedding and the two men headed down South W.W. White Road to search the property surrounding the abandoned farmhouse after the owner granted verbal consent. They hoped but dared not believe they would find the answer to Susan McFarland's disappearance there. It was just another lead to follow—just another patch of ground to cover. They traveled leads down a lot of dead-end roads, like this morning's disappointing dog disinterment and the day they slogged through dense undergrowth to find a deer carcass under the circling of twenty-five buzzards. Both knew it was possible that Susan's body might not ever be found.

Despite their caution, this lead would prove to be the one they had sought for so many days. This scraggly piece of property was the one that contained the charred, abandoned body of Susan McFarland. At last.

The arrest of Rick McFarland was imminent. The first concern was the safety of the children. Representatives of the Texas Department of Protective and Regulatory Services rushed over to the schools where the boys attended their after-school-care programs.

At 4 P.M., Rick called Jennifer Biry at work. A couple of weeks earlier, she had resumed meal delivery at Rick's request. "Are you planning on taking food over to the house this evening?"

"Of course, Rick."

"I wanted to check because of what was printed in the newspaper today," he said referring to an article about a CPS investigation of a life-endangering situation in the McFarland household. I thought you might be afraid I would have the chain saw going."

Although he did not know it, Rick McFarland would not need to worry about dinner that night. Texas Ranger Palmer and Terrell Hills investigator Wedding shadowed his every move as he drove through the streets of San Antonio. As soon as the two officers got word that the three McFarland boys were secure, they made their move to take Rick into custody.

40

Ann Carr flew to St. Louis early on January 14. She did not have time to unpack before the phone call arrived summoning her back to San Antonio.

Sue McFarland was found at last. The children were safe. Palmer and Wedding arrested Rick in the middle of downtown San Antonio. They delivered him to the Bexar county correctional center where he was now behind bars. Relief flooded the senses of Mary Dry, Vanessa Hanes and Kate Kohl at the Heidi Search Center. It was over. The exhaustion they had denied for weeks overtook them as the adrenaline that fueled their efforts faded from their systems.

There was a strong sense of sadness, too. All their hopes for a good outcome died weeks before. But still, the actual confirmation of Sue's death hit them hard. If only a callous Sue had abandoned her home, her husband, her children in the throes of crazed lust. It would mean she was not the sterling Sue that they'd come to know, but she would have been alive. They knew it was a time of mixed emotions for the family—the relief of closure intermingled with the pain of hopeless grief. They ached for them as they moved on to other cases, other families, other searches.

Pete Smith was angry—very angry. Now that his sister was located, he knew the depths of Rick's inhumanity. He knew the intensity of the bottled-up anger and violence Rick had used to cause her death. He knew the callous treatment Rick gave her body after he took her life.

He also knew that Rick had told his parents not to say anything or ask any questions. Pete was baffled that they complied. He thought their behavior was as bizarre as Rick's—all wrapped in a mantle of faith, misusing religion to justify their sins. He could not understand the McFarlands' callous indifference to the fate of one he held so dear.

When he thought about Rick, he remembered the words of a serial killer in one of his investigations: "It's not hard to kill someone. The hardest part is making up your mind to do it."

Pete shuddered when he thought that even that decision was not a difficult one for Rick.

As soon as he was imprisoned, Rick signed a request for protective custody. He stated that due to the highly publicized nature of his case, his life might be in danger in the general population. His request was granted.

After the arrest, Wedding and Palmer returned to 9394 South W.W. White Road at 11 P.M. to relieve the officers on guard. They pulled a tarp over the trailer and strung yellow crime-scene tape between the property and the roadway.

At 2 A.M., they were relieved by Texas Ranger Marrie Garcia and Terrell Hills Police Sergeant Clint Moore, who maintained a security vigil overnight. At 8:30 that morning, Wedding and Palmer were back at the site.

Bexar County Fire Marshall Investigator Ted Manganello took a phone call at 9 A.M. As soon as the immensity of the case hit him, he wished he had never answered the phone. Although later he would be glad he had been part of such an important investigation, on the ride out to the scene, he was anxious about the performance pressure in this media-hot situation and worried about the possibility that he might have to testify at a trial.

As he approached the site with volunteer reserve investigator Anthony Ibarra, his concerns escalated. He expected to see law-enforcement vehicles lining the streets. He had not anticipated the massive invasion of the media. TV news personnel were on top of their satellite trucks in search of a better view. Reporters lounged in lawn chairs with coolers by their sides as if at a tailgate party. They all waited like vultures for the tiniest shred of news to seep out of the investigative enclave.

Manganello and Ibarra rushed to the scene, but now all they could do was wait. To minimize disruption and contamination of evidence, Palmer and Wedding wanted to take all the investigative officers onto the property at the same time. One last team had yet to show.

It was nearly 10 when DPS crime-scene techs led by June Burgett arrived from the crime lab in Austin. Palmer and Wedding led the band of experts through the weeds to the trailer containing the remains of Susan McFarland.

After a flurry of multi-agency photographs was taken, the Bexar County Fire Marshall investigators were the first to take samples. They collected debris around the trailer and a soil sample from the liquid pool at the south end. From the interior, they gathered charred material from different areas, including under Susan's leg and head. They also collected a piece of paper from beneath her head, the melted remains of a cigarette lighter and burned soda cans, as well as samples from the body itself.

Then, the rusty burned remains of a television monitor, a coil of springs from a chair and the charred shell of a VCR were lifted off the body to let the DPS techs do their job. They found plant material on the bumper of the trailer that resembled the botanical samples previously recovered from the front grille of the Suburban and from a pair of socks at the McFarland home.

They collected, bagged and labeled a black rubber glove, Italian Ice wrappers, a pocket knife, a picture frame, buttons, a metal buckle and a metal letter "S." At some point during this process, news helicopters formed an angry-sounding swarm of voyeurs overhead. The team paused long enough to erect a canopy over the trailer to conceal the contents from the intrusive glare of zoom lenses on the cameras.

Manganello and Ibarra lifted the upper torso, including the skull, and placed it on a white sheet. Once it was moved, an arm remained in the spot beneath it. The arm was placed on the sheet with the torso.

They folded the white sheet and placed it inside a body bag. Then they placed that in a gray plastic container. Techs removed two pieces of plastic material—one white, one blue—that had lain under the body.

Obvious bone fragments were plucked from the debris and set down on the other white sheet. After that, personnel sifted the debris in the trailer to collect the smaller pieces of bone. They folded the sheet and placed it inside the second body bag.

Sergeant Palmer taped the gray plastic container shut and added the date and his initials. He applied a piece of tape to the zipper of the second bag, then dated and initialed it, too.

Manganello and Ibarra carried this burden out to the waiting Alamo City Mortuary Services vehicle. The remains were transferred to the Bexar County Medical Examiner's Office for positive identification and autopsy.

At 7337 Louis Pasteur Road, Chief Medical Examiner Dr. Vincent DeMaio discovered two thin gold bands—one set with three stones—on the left ring finger. The inscription inside one of the rings read "RMM to SBS."

Dr. David Senn, forensic dentist, compared Susan's dental records to the X-rays of the remains. He found twenty consistent features and twelve inconsistent features. The latter were the result of trauma inflicted before and after her death. Shawn Palmer's initial assumption was verified. Susan McFarland was no longer missing.

41

District Attorney Susan Reed called a press conference on January 15. Ann Carr declined the invitation to attend. She did, however, want to see it. She went into the neighborhood courthouse bar, but was unable to convince the others gathered there to turn the television to the news. Blanca Hernandez came to the rescue and took Ann to her home to watch the media event there.

At 10 that night, Raul Ruiz watched the local news. He was surprised to see that the body was found near his home. But when they aired a photograph of Rick McFarland, he was shocked. He recognized the man he'd first mistaken for a skinhead—the man standing in front of his Suburban on South W.W. White Road the week of Thanksgiving.

Dr. Randall Frost conducted the autopsy the next morning. He worked with the charred remains, which included a skull, a torso, partial arms and fragments of bone, including leg bones. He found extensive loss of tissue and bone. It appeared as if some of the smaller bones were incinerated in the flames. But there was no indication that any had been removed from the scene.

Some of the internal organs were no longer identifiable. Those that were suffered severe damage from the fire. Although the body was in several pieces, there were no tool marks to indicate any severing of the limbs or the head.

There was a hole in the left side of the head consistent with a skull fracture. Additionally, there were fractured ribs and a fractured spinal column. All of these major fractures occurred while Susan was still alive. No bullets were present in the body.

Susan McFarland died as the result of homicidal violence. The multiple fractures determined the cause of death to be blunt trauma.

Ann met with the district attorney and about fifteen others from the D.A.'s office and law enforcement. The officials all apologized in as many ways as possible when informing Ann that the facts of the case did not warrant the pursuit of the death penalty.

They were all stunned when Ann, the sister of a homicide victim, expressed her relief. Ann went on to explain her strong opposition to the death penalty—even under these personal circumstances. She said that if the death penalty were on the table, it could cause dissension within Sue's family, and right now they needed unity to face their grief and the long ordeal ahead.

On January 17 at 3 P.M. at the Bexar County jail, Sergeant Palmer served Rick McFarland a warrant charging him with murder by injury.

42

That night Rick talked to his mother, who was crying about her fears for the three boys. Rick told her he didn't care about what happened to him, but that "it is the call of my life to insure the kids not live in state custody or in foster homes. I want a Christian home or school."

He urged his mother to use all her assets to pay his brother David and his wife Julie to take the kids. "I can rot in jail. Screw bail. Screw attorneys. Get the kids to David and Julie. It's the only lasting legacy I have control over."

Later he talked to his dad about his other brother and sister-in-law. "Life is over for me. I'm only concerned about the kids. Use all your resources to pay off Don and Debbie to take the kids. I do not want to hear about foster parents for the kids. You need to be proactive."

The next day, he told his mother, "I want to go to my wife's funeral with the kids. I don't care how many people are looking at me cross-eyed."

But Rick was not there when friends and family of Susan McFarland filed into the First Presbyterian Church on Tuesday, January 21, 2003, for Sue's afternoon memorial service. Throughout the gathered crowd, Southwestern Bell corporate identification badges dangled from jackets, dresses and purses.

Beneath the vaulted ceiling studded with heavy carved wood beams, attendees slid into wooden pews topped with red cushions. Light filtered through a variety of elaborate stained-glass windows—Jesus with his apostles looked with compassion on the mourners below.

Reverend Louis Zbinden announced the call to worship, and the bustling ceased, the whispers ended. The silence of the dead stole from pew to pew. The service began with a song and Bible reading. Then Gary Long, Sue's supervisor in the accounting department of Southwestern Bell, stood at the dais. His remarks brought tears and spread rueful chuckles through the audience.

"It is hard to know how to begin to describe Susan. Do you start with her brown coffee cup that said, 'Give Me Chocolate or Give Me Death'? Yes, that was Susan! Do you start with Susan coming in at six A.M. so she could take a long lunch for Junior Achievement or to meet a friend coming in from St. Louis later in the day? Or Susan staying late to make sure the project for the next day was ready to go? Do you start with the daily trip to the ice machine, followed by an afternoon of listening to the crunch of ice for those who sat closest to her? Yes, that was Susan! Do you start with the hours spent on the quarterly balance sheet or the days and weeks figuring out how we were really accounting for Directory operations? Do you start with the frequent trips to the cafeteria to see what the dessert for that day was and whether it had chocolate or not? Do you start with the mornings Susan brought in Shipley Do-Nuts for everyone— the ones with chocolate icing? Yes, that was Susan!

"All of these things describe Susan, but the three words that I think best describe Susan are: Susan loved life.

"[. . .] It is my prayer that we might all remember Susan's sweet spirit and the joy she found in living. I especially pray that her family, in those quiet moments of reflection that will come, might feel of her Spirit and of her love for them and find comfort and peace in knowing that one day they can be re-united with her again."

Friends Blanca Hernandez and Margot Cromack stepped up to run through the alphabet with remembrances of Sue. Sue's brother, Harley Smith, followed the two women. He was 15 years old when his little sister Sue was born on New

Year's Eve, 1958. "In retrospect, it was right that Susie was born on the biggest party night of the year," he said. "Dad called her 'my best little tax deduction.' "

His final words reflected the hearts of many in the church that day. "We mourn your passing, but celebrate the joy you brought to our lives."

In the audience, Kate Kohl of the Heidi Search Center vowed to remain stoic. She tried to practice what she preached to staff and volunteers again and again: "We cannot cry. We cannot get emotionally involved. We need to be the strength and support of the family." Yet, when Kate saw the three motherless boys, a lump formed in her throat. When she focused on little Timmy and knew that his direct memories of his mother would soon fade away, her tears flowed. She would have loved to know Sue—alive, in charge, her arms wrapped around her sons.

As uplifting as the eulogies were, many others were also overcome with sorrow—breaking down in tears with the first refrains of "Amazing Grace." The service ended with final words from Reverend Zbinden: "Although we celebrate her life, we cannot pretend that our world is not darker because Susan's bright light is not shining."

At the reception that followed the service, bright colored balloons filled the room in honor of Sue and "for children of all ages." William, James and Timmy kept busy running around and hiding under tables. But often, William broke away from his brothers to wrap neighbors and family friends with big bear hugs.

After the service, Timmy told his Aunt Ann, "I'm just a little boy and all I have is a bag of bones for a mom."

"You will always have your mom in your heart," Ann assured him.

Timmy thought about that for a moment, then he smiled and said, "You're right. I do."

That conversation broke Ann's heart, but other words she overheard flamed her to anger. In Ann's presence, Mona McFarland said, "Susan didn't have an ounce of mothering instinct in her."

And that was not the only callous, ugly statement Mona made. She even told one person, "The boys' mother was an evil woman." More than once, she told others, "Rick has many, many, many reasons for what he did."

Wesley Miller got off the school bus, came into the house and slumped in a chair. His body limp. His eyes glazed. His face ashen.

His mother Carrie asked, "What's wrong, Wesley?"

He turned to her with moist eyes, "Did Mr. McFarland really burn Mrs. McFarland up?"

Carrie's anger at Rick flared. No young once-innocent boy should ever have to ask a question like that. "Yes he did, Wesley. But he burned her body. She did not feel a thing."

Thirteen-year-old Stephanie Miller dealt with her demons, too. Her bedroom window overlooked the back of the McFarland home and had a clear view into the windows now that the hackberry tree no longer stood in the way. She lowered her blinds and tightened the slats. "I had a murderer looking at me," she said. Her blinds remained that way every day—all day long—for years.

Sue's family held another memorial service in Sue's hometown of Webster Groves on February 1. The start of the service was delayed by the late arrival of Sue's Amarillo friend, Dee Ann Dowlen. Even more fanatical a shopper than Sue, she lost track of time on a side trip to the nearby Saks. It was a story Sue would have loved. It did not, however, amuse some of those who stood in the damp cold waiting for the event to begin.

Sue's high school friend Sandy spoke bittersweet words in celebration of Sue's life. "In the spirit of our fun friend Sue, listen to some Kathy Mattea, try a new recipe, buy some art glass, savor a smiley cookie, get your feet pampered and paint your toenails hot pink, take a spontaneous, unplanned trip somewhere and make it your own adventure du Jour. And when doing these things, most definitely think of Sue and smile.

"In my opinion, if we do some of the things suggested here, we honor Sue's legacy to us—her love of being a mom, her generosity, and her fun nature—and we carry her in our hearts. If we do these things, think of Sue, and smile, then we pass along the joy of life that she personified so well, and she smiles right along with us."

Goodbyes said. Tears shed. It was now time to seek justice for Susan McFarland.

43

Before investigators found Susan's body, botanists Patty Pasztor and Paul Cox performed botanical analysis on the plant samples collected from the Suburban grille and undercarriage, and tape lifts from Rick McFarland's shoes, socks and pants. On January 22, they went to the crime scene on South W.W. White Road.

They cut plants from the roadside, along the worn path leading to the trailer and in a twenty-foot radius to the south of the trailer where Sue's body had rested for weeks. They took care to collect any flowers and seeds and placed each sample in separate one-gallon-sized plastic bags. Each was labeled and numbered. They filled fifteen bags in all. They also collected duplicate specimens in the vicinity of the trailer and taped those in a hard-covered book to press.

At the end of the study of the botanical evidence, they matched seven species of plants from the scene to samples obtained from the stolen Suburban and Rick's clothing—redroot pigweed, yellow wood sorrel, beggars' ticks, hooded windmillgrass, threelobe false mallow, buffelgrass and multi-flowered false rhodesgrass. All of these plants were common in the area. But one burr found at the site and on a sock belonging to Richard McFarland stood out—there was only one area in Bexar County where it could be found, the location where Sue's abandoned, burned body rested for weeks.

• • •

On February 3, Sergeant Palmer talked to the previous owner of 351 Arcadia Place. He learned that there was a remov-
able floor panel inside the closet under the stairs. The panel
allowed access to a crawlspace beneath the house.

Palmer obtained a search warrant and, with Investigator
Julian Martinez from the Bexar County District Attorney's
Office, went back into the McFarland home. When they
cleared away the items stored on the closet floor and lifted
up the cut-out section of the wood flooring, the dirt below
did not appear disturbed. They found no additional evidence
down in that dark hole.

The trip was not a waste, though. They found an interesting hand-written document on top of the desk in Rick's
second-floor office. Rick, it appeared, wrote this suggestion
for a possible defensive strategy before his arrest and before
the discovery of Susan's body:

Framing Theory
She planted evidence before abandoning her family.
Motive 1: To divert attention to Rick to get the police
*   to only search for her locally.*
Motive 2: To eliminate the stigma of the woman who
*   did the unthinkable—abandoned her children.*
Motive 3: Revenge on Rick for not moving out the
*   previous year when Susan asked.*
Motive 4: Her dad was an FBI Agent for 35 years,
*   she must of picked up extensive knowledge about*
*   crime scenes from the stories her father brought*
*   home.*

It took a strange mind to conceptualize this theory. It took
even more distorted thinking to believe the scenario would
find credibility with law enforcement, the district attorney or
even a jury of his peers.

Before his bail-reduction hearing, Rick contacted Steven
Rogers, owner of Alamo Mini Storage, to ask him to be a

witness on his behalf. At Rick's request, Steven called one
of Rick's attorneys.

"Do you think Rick is violent?" the lawyer asked.

"I've never seen him act violently," Steven said.

"Do you think Rick is honest?"

"Rick wanted to store items at my place to keep the police from finding them."

Steven never heard from the legal team again.

On February 7, in district court, Judge Sid Harle presided
over the bail reduction hearing for Richard McFarland. His
bail was now set at $950,000 for four charges: murder, unau-
thorized use of a vehicle, attempting to bribe a witness and
tampering with evidence.

The prosecution argued for no reduction in bail. The defense stated the current bail amount was outrageously high.
They requested a bail of $100,000.

Seventy-three-year-old Dick McFarland testified that his
son was a gentle man who posed no danger to the community and no risk of flight to avoid prosecution. He portrayed
his son as a God-fearing, church-attending father who
"would not run or any of that foolishness because he would
lose his kids if he did."

The judge lowered the bail to $550,000. That meant that
to gain Rick's release from Bexar County jail, his family
would have to raise a minimum $55,000 and possibly have
to post collateral for the rest. Rick's retired parents, living on
fixed incomes, managed to scrape together $30,000—far
short of the amount required.

After the hearing, District Attorney Susan Reed said,
"This case was put together one piece at a time through good
old-fashioned detective work, and when all these pieces are
put together in court, we are confident that McFarland will
be convicted."

44

On February 12, Rick spoke to his mother and told her not to allow Ann Carr into his house. He also said that he did not want Ann to be the executor of Sue's estate.

Rick talked to his dad two days later. Dick told his son that he thought Ann should be allowed into the house. Rick was adamant—she must be denied access. Rick warned his dad about one other person—Charlene Schooling. Rick told Dick not to share anything with her. Charlene, he said, was bad news. Then they discussed the bail. Rick insisted they could get the $55,000 from a bank in St. Louis.

The next day, Mona was upset about borrowing money for the 10 percent needed to bail Rick out of jail. "Who will have to pay the other 90 percent if you don't show up?" she asked.

"The estate will pay," Rick said.

Dick got on the phone and said, "I filed a motion to have Ann as executor. You should use your time for something worthwhile."

"Fuck!" Rick exploded.

"I cannot oppose Ann," Dick continued as if the forbidden word had not been spoken, "because I would have to take the witness stand."

The next week, Rick talked to his dad and expressed his distress that the judge had not yet made a decision on whether or not a simple 10 percent down payment with no additional collateral would be sufficient to bond him out of jail.

"The judge and district attorney are both up for re-election," Dick said.

"Oh, God."

"Unbelievable," Dick agreed.

"I'm not going to make it here much longer," Rick said.

The following day, Rick cried as he begged his mother, "Don't go back to St. Louis till I'm out of jail."

"I don't know what to do," Mona said. "How could this happen? I can't take this."

Rick continued to sob. "Ask any family member to sell property or the house to get bail money."

On Saturday, February 22, Rick told his dad, "This morning, go ahead and process me out as if you don't know any better. Go to the bank and get the big piece of paper—the big fifty-five-K cashier's check—and just make a beeline down here and just show up like everyone else and, just routine, process me out. And the worst thing they can say is, 'I don't think so.' Last Friday, they just couldn't believe I wasn't leaving."

"Are you sure? You sure?"

"So, try it, Dad . . . just go in and play dumb to them."

"Well, what do you mean?"

"It's because they want me out of here. I'll be out in two hours. Do me a favor—humor me—and like you don't know any better, go get the big piece of paper, come down and just say, 'I'm here to bail out my son.' "

"Well . . ."

"Let's just see what happens."

"Well, first off, talking to this guy at the bonds in the first-floor window down there . . ."

Rick interrupted, "Okay, when you say you are here to pick up Rick, here's the fifty-five thousand . . ."

"Okay but first they have to check to see if the judge has that on the statement—the ten percent factor—if we don't, that'll shut it down right there unless they really screw up."

"Yeah, that's what I was going to say, explore, just try it," Rick pleaded.

Dick, however, was not willing to play games with the authorities in the hopes that they would make a mistake.

In March, Rick told his parents that he wanted a visit from Chaplain Al Logan, the director of detention ministries. The chaplain could bring in two books. "I want *Winning in the Cash Flow Business* and *Tin Can Alley: How to Make Money* ASAP. Tell the jail people I want to speak with Al Logan. Don't tell them about the books though."

Mona had reservations about dealing with Logan. She did not feel he was good enough to visit with her son.

In early March, David McFarland penned a letter to his brother Rick while sitting in the Macaroni Grill waiting for his order of Penne Rustica to arrive:

> *Every time I am enjoying the outdoors or some other luxury I used to take for granted, I think about you and where you are[. . .] I can't believe I'm actually writing a letter like this to a brother who is in prison.*
>
> *[. . .] The fact is I cannot save you or William, James and Timmy. That's the bad news, the Great News is that I know the one that can save you and the boys and I pray that the Holy Spirit would indwell you and the boys so you would have the same assurance.*

He then wrote about his reluctance to follow the plan cooked up by Rick and his mom to pretend to be adopting the children when he and his wife had no intention of keeping them more than a couple of months. He expressed his concern about the legal consequences of taking this action:

> *If anyone can understand the fears of messing with the State of Texas and their legal system, it would be you! So it is with a heavy heart that I must tell you that Julie and I will not be taking any part in a*

*home-study. I hope you can understand that my first
and foremost obligation is to my family.*

Mona and Dick had two accounts at the Bank of America in
Missouri—a checking account and a home equity line of
credit that was created to be overdraft protection for the first
account. A couple years before, the elder McFarlands
stopped hearing about the accounts, but were not concerned.
They were inactive accounts and they thought the $19 bal-
ance they left in the checking account eroded to nothing because of the $5 monthly service fee.

Behind bars, Rick was unable to cover his tracks by making the payments necessary to keep the account alive and
keep everyone unaware of what he had done. Back in December of 2000, Rick used his father's Social Security number to gain access to the account. He changed the address
from St. Louis to a mail drop box in San Antonio that he
opened in the name of Ramona McFarland.

Rick forged over $28,000 worth of checks in 2001 and
more than $15,000 in 2002. On top of that, he rang up thou-
sands of dollars on the check card at CompUSA, OfficeMax,
Wal-Mart, Target, Wolf Camera, Alamo Heights Office Supply, Eckerd drug, The Sharper Image, Sprint and Paris
Hatters.

Helping his wife, Ann, review all the paperwork that
might be attached to Sue's estate, Gary Carr uncovered the
trail of theft—Rick left the elder McFarlands with $59,670.96
worth of debt on their home equity line of credit.

Dick and Mona had stood by their son. They believed in
him. Rick accepted everything they offered him—and never
hesitated to ask for more. All the while, he knew he'd ripped
them off and destroyed any vestige of financial stability they
had in their old age.

Did Rick apologize or show any remorse for what he had
done? Of course not. He told his parents, "Sue made me do
the Bank of America thing."

Mona accepted this excuse. Either she really believed
him or she could not cope with believing anything else.

Dick seemed a bit more skeptical about his son and money in a conversation he and Mona had with Rick a few days later.

"Go to H-E-B and get a three-hundred-dollar check sent to the P.O. Box," Rick said.

"Why three hundred dollars? I've been sending one hundred dollars."

"I said three hundred dollars! Take it out of my house."

"How do we do that?" Mona asked.

"My brain is not in very good shape."

Dick insisted he was only going to send $100 to Rick's fund at the prison. Rick countered with an offer of $200. Dick finally expressed his disgust; "You've been spending it before you got it for forty years."

Charlene Schooling felt mighty sorry for Dick and Mona. It had gotten so hard to be the parents of Rick McFarland. She offered to bring dinner over to them after they got home from visiting Rick in jail. When they arrived at 351 Arcadia, Charlene trooped over with a casserole, a salad and a pitcher of iced tea.

Mona was sitting on a sofa in the living room with the Bible opened on her lap. Charlene put the food in the kitchen and sat down next to her.

Mona said, "Susan was a horrible mother."

Charlene was stunned—but still compassionate. "No, Susan really was a good mother," she assured her.

"Rick worked so hard around here."

Charlene sure didn't remember that, but she did not want to attack this already beleaguered woman. "I never saw him much," was all that she said.

"Susan liked to shop at that Central Market because Susan always had to have the best."

Charlene explained that a lot of women in the neighborhood shopped there on a regular basis. It was close, convenient and a good source for prepared foods for a quick dinner.

"Did Susan ever cook?"

"She was a great cook. She baked cookies for the boys all the time," Charlene said in defense of her friend.

"See that pillow over there?" Mona said pointing to the Mary Englebreit pillow bearing the legend "IT'S GOOD TO BE QUEEN." "That's exactly what Susan thought. Nothing was ever good enough for her."

Charlene was speechless.

"If she wanted to have a career, why did she have kids?" Mona asked.

Charlene wanted to snap back and tell her that if her lazy son had held a job, maybe Susan could have stayed home. But she held her peace and said her goodbyes.

By the time she reached her home, all the sympathy she had for Rick's parents had turned to dust. She brushed it away and had nothing more to do with either of them.

45

In a conversation with his parents, Rick said, "I trust communication goes to David to keep the kids out of a foster home. The proper paperwork needs to be filed."

"David understands the custody hearing," Mona said. "He's spoken with the social workers."

"What's David up to?"

"David is coming to the Friday hearing, but they are not able to take any of the kids."

"David doesn't want the kids' custody?" Even though David had told him so, Rick did not believe it. His voice shook with the shock as if it were a new revelation. "My brain is fried."

"Don, David and Julie are talking to Christian homes that can accommodate the kids' needs."

David talked to Rick right before the hearing. "The kids have gone through enough heartache. No more false hopes—they need a permanent home."

"What do you mean?" Rick asked.

"We need to be prepared for the worst. Julie and I are not capable of handling the reality—of dealing with it."

"This whole thing sucks."

"I can't wave a wand and save you and the kids. The bottom line is, we're not taking custody of the kids," David said.

"How about temporary custody—eighteen months?"

"I'm not going to bring a child into my home on a temporary basis and then let him go."

"I cannot comprehend why you won't help," Rick said.

With a trial not scheduled for quite some time, the public's
attention turned to Sue's children. The two younger boys
were placed with a foster family and the oldest boy was in a
facility with programs and staff specializing in counseling
troubled and traumatized kids.

Rick was fighting to maintain custody of his children. By
law, he was innocent until proven guilty, making it necessary
for the legal process to plod its way forward on the subject
of custodial rights.

He told his parents to move the kids to St. Louis and put
them in a Nazarene or Baptist children's home in Missouri.
"I do not want my kids in a Texas foster home."

In another conversation, Dick asked Rick where they
could find the children's birth certificates. If anyone adopted
the boys, they'd need those.

"The point is to get the kids out of state and up in St.
Louis. Don't mess it up," Rick responded.

CPS laid out a family service plan that included psychological evaluation for Rick as well as his attendance at parenting classes. In a late March hearing, Rick's lawyer
argued that the plan was designed to set McFarland up for
defeat. Judge Peter Sakai overruled her, insisting on compli-
ance if Rick wanted full rights with the boys.

After the hearing, his attorney told the media, "He
doesn't want to comply with the treatment plan, nor could he
because he is incarcerated."

The boys' future remained up in the air. Rick's parents
had physical limitations that prohibited the adoption of the
children. Rick's brothers made no indication that they were
interested in pursuing it. The family lawyer expressed their
hope that Rick would be exonerated and reunited with his
children.

Sue's family was not entertaining that possibility at all.
They were listening to the advice of CPS workers who

assured them that the best interest of the boys was to remain in their current stable situation until the guilt or innocence of their father was determined. They believed this appraisal and, regardless, didn't think the courts would sanction any other course of action at this time. They did not realize that long-term placement in a foster home gave the foster parents as much power in determining the future of the children as any of the family members.

While they waited, Sue's family considered their options for the future. Although the state had taken a position that the boys should all stay together, they questioned the advisability of that proposition. It might be preferable for each boy to be in a separate home—homes where they could get the intense one-on-one care they needed.

Because of the age difference between Sue and her three older siblings, her sister and brothers were beyond the child-rearing stage and were now welcoming grandchildren into their lives. Nonetheless, Ann and her husband Gary were still willing to adopt one of the boys. Kirsten, closer to Sue's age, was a single mother—her hands full with the responsibilities of raising her two children and supporting their household.

They did, however, want all of the children placed with blood relatives. They wanted the boys to remain part of their lives, to be grounded in the security of a shared family history. While they searched for good alternatives within their own family, they also reached out to Rick's relatives. Ann talked to both of Rick's brothers, Don and David, about the possibility. She made sure they knew that Sue's estate was substantial enough to provide the necessary financial assets to help raise the children and that Sue's siblings were willing to help with some additional funds if needed. But neither of Rick's brothers would consider adopting even one of the boys.

Ann was disappointed—but what did she expect? Neither of the brothers had been eager to help out with the difficult situation in San Antonio in any tangible way. When Ann asked David to assume the responsibility for finding a home for Sally the dog, he said, "I don't want to do that." He never offered to do anything else in exchange.

On April 2, 2003, Sergeant Palmer visited Rick McFarland in his jail cell. He delivered the official charges to the prisoner. Count one: Rick was charged with offering "to confer a benefit upon Richard Clemmer, specifically the purchasing of a dinner, if Richard Clemmer would withhold information from law enforcement." The second count reiterated the dinner offer "if Richard Clemmer would testify falsely."

The final charges were murder/murder by injury, accusing that McFarland "did then and there intending to cause serious bodily injury to an individual, Susan McFarland, commit an act clearly dangerous to human life, its manner and means unknown to the grand jury, thereby causing the death of Susan McFarland against the peace and dignity of the state."

Rick would not drop his insistence that his brother David and sister-in-law Julie pursue adoption under false pretenses. On May 7, David and Julie each sent him a letter.

David elaborated on conversations with attorney Laura Heard regarding the concerns he had expressed in an earlier letter:

> Laura Heard said it's not that _easy_ to just drop a child off and say it didn't work out. She said family services could accuse you of child abandonment and your own kids could be at risk _of being removed._
>
> I have cut out part of a letter that was sent to mom and dad from Laura H. explaining it. _I'm not making this up._
>
> Rick you must understand where we are coming from. Besides, there are other issues. We are stressed to the max with our own kids and a new puppy! We are concerned what this would do to _our family_ and _marriage._ We are not equipped to handle the

emotional trauma of what they have been through.
    [. . .] The bottom line is whoever does a home
study needs to be sincere about permanent custody!
<u>*Not for one month!*</u>

Julie did not frame her letter with the words of love and
compassion that filled her husband's letter to Rick. She was
far more blunt:

This serious family problem has affected each of us
very personally. Susan is dead—maybe eternally, the
boys have been robbed of a mother and a father, and
you are jailed. Your parents struggle to survive each
day not understanding what is going on. And even
David, me and our kids suffer. In an effort to protect
me and the kids, David had been doing what I refer to
as the "McFarland Crap"—lying or not fully disclos-
ing information, mail, etc. I know this is a staple of
the Rick and Susan relationship AND the Don and
Debra relationship. I refuse to have a relationship
short of best friends, soulmates. To that end I am writ-
ing to you to fully disclose my feelings and intentions.
    Your family has always been a challenge—lack of
boundaries, constant bickering, half-truths. Your chil-
dren have been suffering for years and now are ulti-
mately suffering worse than I ever imagined.
    After much counseling and discussion, our house-
hold will not apply for temporary, permanent, semi-
permanent, etc. custody of the boys. I realize our
decision may put you at risk of losing your parental
rights. What incredible guilt!! Whose guilt? The an-
swer lies inside of you—David and I are not to blame
for the consequences of your actions. Please note we
have attempted to pour out unconditional love to
you—whether you are guilty or innocent of destroying
Susan and your family.
    It is quite difficult to watch you remain silent—
using your Christian-ese—either proclaim your true

*innocence before us all or show sorrow and remorse
and move toward forgiveness.*

She then ordered him not to mention the custody of the
boys in any future correspondence with David.

46

Rick received a letter from his father in early June that explained the rules requiring both cash and collateral to bail him out of jail. Dick explained his fears about signing over their house, vehicles and IRA accounts to the court.

Then his letter turned to the Bank of America situation. "We are so sorry that this creative financing got out of hand. We are still devastated as much as you are."

After being ripped off for more than $60,000, Dick offered sympathy instead of rebuke to his son.

A few days later, a letter arrived from Mona. She talked about a downturn in Dick's health and chatted about the latest news. Then she lashed out at Sue's family.

> Dad talked with Gary Carr one day the other week and Gary was saying that the surviving spouse is responsible for all debts. Ann wants you to pay half of the house mortgage and she pays the other half; we suggest that you not sign any papers to that effect. Because, we feel that you will not get a nickel out of the sale of the house, because the Smiths and Carrs will see-to-it that you do not get anything. At least, that is our thinking and feeling now. The Smiths and Carrs being lawyers know the angles and how to dodge around the truth. Sorry to say.
>
> Anyway, again we must trust the LORD to work out the details.

• • •

Rick did not adjust well to time behind bars. In June, Officer Ledesma conducted a pat-down search before returning him from the law library to his cell. He found two Jolly Rancher candies inside Rick's left sock. This was a violation of simple facility regulations.

At his disciplinary hearing, Rick said, "They were in my sock. It was impossible for me to remove them. I normally carry them in my sock because my radio is in my pocket. I forgot to take them out. Ledesma came down. I was lying down. I heard, 'C'mon, hurry up.' I didn't get called til 11:05. I was supposed to go at 10:55. I was told by another inmate that Ledesma socialized with another officer on my time. How much time am I supposed to get to get ready?"

Rick found no sympathy. His phone, visitation and commissary privileges were removed for four days.

On August 7, Rick's cellmate, Max Castillo, informed an officer that he and McFarland were not getting along and might end up fighting. Castillo said that McFarland would not stop accusing him of stealing his commissary and he was sick of it.

When McFarland was questioned, he said that he had not reported the theft to staff, but he had other inmates in the unit keeping an eye on his cell to see what was going on. He insisted that he knew Castillo took his stuff when Rick went to the law library. He asked that Castillo be relocated to prevent any further escalation of the problem.

Castillo asked that he and McFarland be listed as enemies. The inmates were separated.

Later that month, Rick's new cellmate Kerns complained that McFarland woke him up in the middle of the night and kept him from sleeping by making a lot of noise. And, he said, McFarland kept the cell dirty. McFarland, on the other hand, said he had no problem with Kerns. Kerns was relocated.

In September, a lieutenant distributing inmates' mail noticed a note addressed to the unit officer slide under the door. It read:

You better get the inmate in Cell 13, McFarland, move before it's too late, because we're going to take care of it ourselfes [sic].

Problems with staff and inmates continued throughout McFarland's stay at the Bexar County Correctional facility.

47

In late July, Rick wrote to his ailing father.

*Just got your handwritten letter that you wrote from
St. Joseph's Hospital. It means so much to me that
you can say that you still love me as a son. I've got
tears in my eyes as I write this, Pops. I feel so re-
morseful how my life is affecting and infecting yours
and so many other people's lives in so many different
ways. Daddy, what should I do?*

August was a dismal month for Rick McFarland. He had
applied to be part of the PATCH—Papas and Their
Children—program at the county jail. Participation required
prisoners to attend a class every day to learn about better
parenting skills, nutrition, personal hygiene and other matters important to their ability to raise a child after their release. Attendance in classon each week earned the inmate a
one-hour contact visit with any and all of their children ages
1 month to 16 years.

On the second of the month, Rick learned that he was not
approved. The security issues involved in contact visits prohibited participation for those men who face drug-dealing or
murder charges or who are known to be gang members.

A harder blow hit Rick on August 7—his father passed
away. Mona called the jail and asked that Rick be allowed
to call her and that a chaplain be provided. "He will

need someone to lean on and will need a lot of comforting."

Jail officials permitted that call as well as another one that Rick placed to one of his brothers. Daryl Christian, the chaplain from Wayside Ministries visited him that same day.

Rick was outraged that he could not go to St. Louis with his boys to his father's funeral. Instead, a CPS caseworker and the court-appointed foster father accompanied William and James. The boys' foster mother remained in Texas with Timmy, who she decided was too young to go to the services. His Aunt Ann wondered why Timmy could not come up and visit with the family even if he did not attend the funeral.

Rick wrote a eulogy for his father that, in his absence, was read to the crowd of mourners by another family member. From the pen of a wife-killer, the final words of the missive were heavy with a message of faith and love:

> *I was most privileged last summer in July 2002 while visiting my family in St. Louis to confirm in person my knowing that my dad is a Christian, a saved child of God. I had* him *explain to me that the key to Heaven's Gate is not earned by earthly good works or because he was a good citizen. Dad verbalized then prayed with me that he yieldingly accepted the gift of God's salvation, by him not earning but receiving the Lord Jesus Christ's Saving Grace.*
>
> *We both put a navy style double square-knot on Dad's Life Eternal Confirmation.*
>
> *What a classic Dad.*
>
> *What a friend.*
>
> *What a guy.*
>
> *What a blessing for all of us who came in close contact with Richard Lyle McFarland.*
>
> *He was a man of few words.*
>
> *He was a man of uplifting actions.*
>
> *Such was my Dad's earthly life. Gosh, I am going to so very truly miss his presence down here. I really look forward to catching up with Dad in Heaven. Daddy, I love you so much.*

The Smith family wondered where that faith was on the night Rick murdered Sue.

While they were in town, Ann took the boys out to the cemetery where Sue was interred. They talked about how wonderful their grandfather looked in his naval officer uniform complete with ceremonial sword. They wanted to know if their mom was beautiful in her casket. Honesty forced Ann to tell them that their mother's body was cremated.

William and James blanched with horror. "You burned up our mother?"

Ann paled, inwardly cursed Rick and then explained. "I know that is what your mother would have wanted. We talked about cremation after our mom died last year." She then quoted scripture about ashes to ashes and the boys seemed willing to accept what happened.

Thank God, Ann thought, that for the moment, they were unaware of what their father did to their mother's body before she was found. She knew they would find out one day. She hoped they would have the emotional maturity to cope with it when that time came.

There was no headstone on Sue's gravesite yet, but Ann pointed to the patch of ground where she rested. "Here's your mom. She's buried next to her mom and dad."

"Where are you going to put my dad?" James asked.

Ann froze. How could she answer this question without causing pain? "Well," she said, "your dad's not dead, so we don't have to worry about that right now, do we?"

"Okay," James said. "Did you notice that there's grass and dirt on your mom and dad's stones?"

"I think they were just through here mowing and it flew up on them."

"Grandma Smith wouldn't like that," James said.

Ann smiled and thought, no, she wouldn't like it one bit.

Together, they brushed the debris off of the stones.

At the end of August, Mona sent her son another letter. She complained about a sinus infection and encouraged Rick to send a birthday card to James. She wrote that she sent her grandson a card with ten $1 bills in it, but would not honor Rick's request to send James a Game Boy Advance cartridge.

Then the Bank of America situation raised its ugly head again.

> As you know by this time, Don and David just found out about the B/A deal. They are both very upset about it which is certainly understandable, and it has caused me a lot of stress also. I am so very sorry that it had to happen. Just exactly how did this thing get started?

Somehow—perhaps from his mother—Rick managed to obtain the telephone number of the foster family who cared for James and Timmy. Against court orders, he dialed it on Christmas Day. The foster mother answered the call. She was torn. She knew she shouldn't allow him to talk to the boys. But it was Christmas. What harm could it do?

She regretted that decision faster than she made it. As soon as Timmy heard the sound of his father's voice, he blanched, dropped the phone and ran to his room. Behind the slammed door, he went into a tormented rampage of destruction. The foster mother never made that mistake again.

Rick still continued to create problems at the Bexar County Correctional Center. On January 5, 2004, Inmate Quinton Moody reported that there would be problems if he and McFarland remained in the same unit. Their conflict started when they were in the BA unit together and now resumed in unit BB. Moody claimed McFarland was going out of his way to make things difficult for him and other prisoners. On January 8, Gregorio Rodriguez claimed he feared for his safety around McFarland.

Later that month, Cecil Burley, McFarland's then-current roommate, said that Rick was flushing stuff down the commode for two days prior to the surprise health, sanitation and contraband inspection of the cell. "He knew something was coming," he said.

Maybe so. But, once again, Rick did not do a thorough job cleaning up the evidence. Inspectors confiscated several non-privileged items, including correspondence, from his cell that day.

Finally in February, after months of motions, delays and the juggling of conflicting schedules, a date was set for the big show. The timing could not have been worse for Sergeant Boyd Wedding. Every February, he took vacation days so he could work at the San Antonio Stock Show and Rodeo—a major event on the city's calendar of events since 1950.

For some, the rodeo was just another excuse for San Antonio to throw a party. It was more than that to serious rodeo fans. The event was inducted into the PRCA—Professional Rodeo Cowboys Association—ProRodeo Hall of Fame in 2003 and was ranked as one of the top five rodeos in the nation. Over one million visitors enter the grounds annually. While there, they consume nearly 5000 pounds of brisket and over 6000 gallons of soda.

One of the big draws every year was the musical talent amassed for the two-week event. 2004 was no exception—including performances by Reba McEntire, Brooks & Dunn, Alan Jackson, Martina McBride, and Dwight Yoakam. Even Willie Nelson was booked, but laryngitis kept him off the stage.

During the days before the trial, Wedding spent his vacation working the rodeo, fielding calls from the district attorney's office, and finding copies of whatever document might be needed. On top of that, anticipation of facing cross-examination added to the stress, and reliving the memories of Sue's disappearance and death resurrected the pain. Some vacation.

The defense's successful change of venue motion moved the trial three counties away to the city of Austin in Travis County. The University of Texas School of Law would host the unfolding drama in a cherrywood-trimmed, state of the art courtroom in the John B. Connally Center for Justice.

The lavish courtroom included a $60,000 bulletproof judge's bench, high-backed leather chairs for the attorneys and a fully equipped TV production studio. With eight cameras to shoot all the action, they would broadcast gavel-to-gavel live coverage on the university's website.

Staff and students coordinated logistics with the District Court in Bexar County and with a bevy of media representatives including reporters and producers from NBC and Court TV. Seventy-nine county residents received the call to report for jury duty on Thursday, February 5, 2004.

The gathered legal talent for the trial was impressive. The defense team was Mark Stevens and Pat Hancock, who between them represented many clients in high-profile cases, including the death penalty appeal for serial killer Tommy Lynn Sells and the criminal trial of Nelson Antonio Escalero, who held San Antonio Archbishop Patrick Flores hostage in his own church.

The state matched them for talent. First Assistant District Attorney Michael Bernard—second only in the department to DA Susan Reed—led the prosecution team. In a previous incarnation, Bernard was an ACLU attorney who represented Branch Davidian members after the fiery fiasco in Waco. When he switched to the other side of the courtroom, he got a guilty verdict on the murder-conspiracy charges against millionaire Allen Blackthorne in the bloody homicide-for-hire perpetrated on Shelia Bellush, Blackthorne's ex-wife, the mother of his daughters and now, in a second marriage, the mother of toddler quadruplets.

Bernard was backed by lawyers Catherine Babbitt, the shining star of domestic violence prosecutions, and Bettina Richardson, whose organizational skills and intense recall of detail kept the team organized and focused. When they got frustrated or off-track, Richardson reminded them, "You eat an elephant one bite at a time."

The state was ready and confident. They had tracked down every issue until it resulted in meaningful evidence or led to a dead end. They even conducted an extensive search for any indication of the presence of a boyfriend and found nothing.

They expected that McFarland's lawyers might claim self-defense or even an accident—he pushed her, she fell down the stairs and he panicked. But the prosecution felt that the evidence surrounding the stolen Suburban would defeat any arguments in that direction. The only viable defense they saw was an insanity plea, but in order to effect that, Rick's attorneys would have to give advance notice of intent, and that had not been forthcoming.

From the state's viewpoint, the most intriguing testimony involved Rick's electronic trail as he hacked into Susan's computer, and that definitive plant burr on Rick's sock. The most compelling evidence they thought they had was the blood in the bathroom, Sue's forcibly removed hair in the back cargo area of the Suburban and the blood on the bumper and the rear locking mechanism of that vehicle. Overall, they believed everything pointed to Rick McFarland from the first time he opened his mouth.

Maybe the most damning evidence of all was the statement made by William about the earring, the shoe and the blood at 356 Arcadia. Although there was nothing in that house, it took no great leap of imagination to understand that William may very well have seen what he described in his very own home.

Nonetheless, the prosecution decided months before that this testimony would not be heard by a jury. The state would not further traumatize any of the three boys by putting them in the witness stand to condemn their father.

48

The prosecution team expected the trial to last three weeks to a month. They did not expect that the defense would call witnesses—McFarland had no true friends, and to call the defendant himself would be a reckless temptation of fate.

Reporters and spectators sat in their seats waiting for the jury selection process to begin. The start time came and went. The minutes dragged by as reporters struck up idle conversation with one another wondering if the delay was significant or just jumbled logistics.

Finally, Rick McFarland entered the courtroom in a blue suit and coordinated tie. His facial expression was flat—no emotion was revealed in his eyes. The weight of reality bore down heavy on his shoulders. Once again, he failed to achieve the goal he set. He did not commit the perfect murder. He dug himself into another hole and Sue—the one person who always came to his rescue—was no longer there to bail him out.

Judge Sid Harle mounted the bench. Defense and prosecuting attorneys announced a plea agreement to a stunned audience. After a moment of silence, the room came back to life—laptops clacked, pens scratched and cameras zoomed in on the players.

According to the deal, the defendant waived his right to a jury trial on the murder charge that carried a possible sentence of 5 to 99 years, and the state dropped the related lesser charges. McFarland lost custody of his sons, but would not be required to offer an explanation of how he killed Susan McFarland. He accepted a sentence of 40 years and would not be eligible for parole until he served 50 percent of the time.

"You are bound to this agreement if I follow it," Judge Harle told McFarland. "You cannot appeal."

The judge turned to the defense team. "Mr. Stevens and Mr. Hancock, is he competent to offer a plea at this time?"

When the lawyers responded in the affirmative, Richard McFarland said the word everyone awaited; "Guilty."

"Are you pleading guilty because you are guilty and for no other reason?" the judge asked.

The defendant said he was. The judge accepted the plea by berating McFarland for his lack of remorse and his indifference to the searchers who scoured the city for his wife. "As far as I am concerned, you have earned a special place in hell."

The prepared statement of Sue's family was then read into the record.

> *Justice is served today. Susan's family can now close this chapter of her life and begin a new chapter—the lead characters being her three beautiful sons. Family and friends have been spared the giving and reliving of the lengthy, horrible parade of evidence marshaled by law enforcement and prosecutors proving Rick McFarland's responsibility for Susan's death—the realization of our worst fears.*
>
> *We are saddened that her sons have now truly lost both their mother and their father, but we are encouraged and sustained by the innumerable acts of kindness, assistance and compassion with which we have been blessed, especially those fine caregivers for the children. We thank and congratulate the prosecutors and law enforcement for their long, hard work—their diligence and dedication—to bring this tragedy to a resolution.*
>
> *Please keep Susan's children and the family of Carmen Alcaraz, which suffers especially at this time, in your prayers.*

Carmen, an Hispanic woman, disappeared a month before Susan McFarland, but her body had not been found for fifteen months. Her funeral was in two days. The effort to solve Carmen's missing persons case did not seem as energetic or focused as that employed in Sue's disappearance. This disparity created an outcry in the community blaming racism as the cause.

Law enforcement, however, pointed to a different reason. They credited Ann Carr with keeping the media spotlight shining with firmness and intensity on Sue's disappearance. That illumination caused the public to be more forthcoming with tips and more willing to volunteer for the searches. They believed if it were not for Ann's efforts, they might never have found the body of Susan McFarland.

Sue's family ended this part of their ordeal with an intense gratitude for the exemplary performance of all the investigators involved in the case, and with Sergeant Palmer in particular. Pete Smith, with both a professional and personal interest in this case, was able to study Shawn Palmer's voluminous report of the investigation. Pete was impressed by its thoroughness. In his opinion, Palmer left no stone unturned. "Even in hindsight," he said, "I could see nothing that could have—or should have—been done differently."

Down in San Antonio, Sergeant Wedding drove along in one of the rodeo trucks. By his side was another stack of papers he had to take to the district attorney's office for delivery to Austin.

He turned up the volume on the radio when the programming was interrupted for breaking news. Rick McFarland pled guilty. Wedding pulled to the side of the road, got out in the middle of the street and screamed with joy.

The scene was much grimmer in the office of a child therapist. There, William, James and Timmy heard of their father's plea. They learned that their dad admitted he killed their mother. They found out that he accepted a serious sentence and would be going away for a long time.

The boys were stunned—James was the most conspicuous

in his distress. Their fate was still in the hands of others. They would not know what their future held until a decision was reached in a Bexar County courtroom in the hearing to terminate their father's parental rights on April 12.

Since his arrest, the boys only saw their father once, when they'd visited him in jail. Now they would not see him again for the remainder of their childhood. At this moment, that thought was incomprehensible.

49

The legal teams that geared up for a performance before a jury—and the world—could not disengage from their adversarial positions when the job was done without the stress-relieving drama of a trial. Stevens and Hancock took exception to District Attorney Susan Reed's remarks to the press—particularly her assertion that the defense proposed the deal only the night before. They went over the top when *San Antonio Express News* columnist Ken Rodriguez printed lead prosecutor Michael Bernard's description of the suddenness of the deal as being "like my worst enemy going off a cliff in my new Ferrari."

The defense attorneys fired off a letter to Michael Bernard.

Nobody in recent times has been portrayed more negatively in our county than Richard McFarland. It is not at all surprising that your boss would go to great lengths to put her best spin on any plea bargain reached with a person so unpopular.

The letter continued with a blow-by-blow account of the defense version of events. Their chronology began in mid-January and included the accusation that Bernard was the first person to mention the possibility of a 40-year sentencing deal.

You're the only one in the county who could have convinced Susan Reed to participate in this plea bargain,

*and, for whatever reason, you did so. If you really
wanted a trial as badly as you led Rodriguez to believe, we would be trying the case right now. If your
brand new Ferrari went off the cliff, you were in the
driver's seat.*

Michael Bernard fired back a response—forgetting in his
moment of ire that the letter he wrote would become part of
the public record.

*Apparently this is getting personal. [. . .] There was
no reason for you to take personal offense or to make
personal attacks.
    [. . .] There certainly was no attack made against
you. There was no "record" which needed to be set
straight. Your integrity was not questioned. No one
was gloating.
    You stated that you exhaustively prepared your
case and properly represented your client. You did,
and no one has suggested otherwise. We prepared
ours. Both of us were ready and willing to proceed.
[. . . I]n the end both sides exercised their professional judgment regarding the resolution of the case.
The case got resolved; the lingering adrenaline takes
a little longer.
    I was and am shocked and surprised your client ac-
tually pled, but do not give a tinker's damn how it
came about. [. . .] I respond only because we were
friends; the depth of your vituperation is bewildering.
I believe the agreement was in the best interest of the
family and fulfills their needs; I believe it to be in the
interest of this community. Clearly you and your client
believed it to be in his best interest. That is the stuff of
which pleas are made. The rest of it is bullshit.*

The public revelation of this spat was embarrassing to all
parties. On the other hand, for the community—rumbling
with the tension caused by the dramatic buildup for the trial

and stunned by the suddenness of its culmination—the squabble was great comic relief.

But the story was not over yet. Everyone held their collective breath as the fate of three innocent, traumatized boys dangled in the breeze.

50

Before going into court on April 12, 2004, Jodi, the foster
mother caring for the two youngest McFarland boys, spoke
to James explaining the day ahead. "Now, we have to start
all over again," she told him.

"I don't want to start over again," James said.

"But this will be the last time, James, and it will be good."

"And I'm never going to get married."

"That will be your decision, James. No one else's."

In the wake of that troubling conversation, the boys' foster mother entered the courtroom of Judge Barbara Nellermoe with a herd of lawyers and other interested family and
friends. Every party concerned about the outcome had an attorney representing their cause sitting at the front tables.

Although the three young boys—the focus of the morning's hearing—were not there, their father was. He entered
the courtroom in a navy jacket, khaki pants, white shirt and
blue patterned tie. Handcuffs, fastened in front of his body,
completed his ensemble.

When Rick took his seat, the cuffs were removed. His
shoulders slumped and the corners of his mouth sagged to
his chin. McFarland's attorney produced an affidavit of relinquishment of parental rights. Rick was sworn in and allowed to make his statement.

"I, Richard McFarland, state on the record that I
freely and willingly gave up my parent rights over my children. [. . .] I am signing for one reason and one reason alone,

so that my children can turn the page and live in a loving home. [. . .] I want them to be together.

"I express the utmost remorse to my three boys, William, James and Timothy. There is nothing I can do to change what has occurred but I want my boys to know that I relinquished my rights because I love them so very much.

"[. . .] I wish love, happiness and growth for my boys in their new home." He then spoke of the boys' foster parents. "Thanks," he said, "for the wonderful care they have given my boys. I'm grateful that I will be able to have contact with the boys in the future with pictures and updates."

McFarland then quoted Proverbs 3:5–6: "Trust in the Lord with all thine heart; and lean not unto thine own understanding. In all thy ways acknowledge him, and he shall direct thy paths."

"Lord knows," he added, "I've been leaning on him a lot lately." His last words galled and infuriated many of the spectators in the room.

After this statement, Shannon Rader-Brooks spoke on behalf of Child Protective Services. "I believe these children have been deprived of their natural parents through the actions of their father. They need to have security and stability of parents for guidance and support in a home.

"Closure is important in their grief. They need to adjust to the loss of the mother and the loss of their father." She then noted that the boys would be 32, 30 and 26 years old when McFarland has his first opportunity for parole. "They have begun recovery, but it is going to be a long process. Only time will tell."

Ann Carr stepped forward next, echoing the desire for the children to be able to start their lives anew. Then she turned her comments to Rick: "He led them to believe that the children might be in some way responsible for their mother leaving. They need to move on to learn to trust, hope and love again."

Rick's attorney requested a final visit between the boys and their father. The boys' attorney voiced a strong objection. Rick's attorney then said, "A goodbye visit is normal. It will help them get closure. The therapist says this is a good thing."

The representative for the district attorney's office admitted that this kind of visit is customary, but objected to it just the same. Her objections were seconded by the boys' attorney and the attorney representing Sue McFarland's family.

Squabbling finished, Judge Nellermoe made a quick decision. "There is clear and convincing evidence to terminate the parental rights of Richard McFarland and it is in the best interests of the children."

Turning to McFarland, Nellermoe added, "There are very few gifts you can give your children, and this relinquishment of rights is one of them. Seeing them again should be the choice of the children. They can do so as adults."

The end of this formality cleared the way for the boys to find the safety and security they needed to heal and grow. In New Jersey, Sue's childhood friend Sandy Riggs explored the possibility of adopting all three boys—she was already Timmy's godmother. At the time, Sandy and her husband and children were in the process of moving back to St. Louis. Both families, and Rick, were supportive of this couple. They both looked into their hearts long and hard. They considered the impact on their own children—one of whom was a special needs child who required an extraordinary amount of attention. In the end, although they wanted to provide a home for Sue's boys, they decided it would not be fair to their kids.

In Georgia, a married cousin of Sue McFarland agreed to adopt James and Timmy. Sue's sister Ann talked with the couple at great length. She wanted them to understand the depth and breadth of this responsibility before they assumed it. She wanted them to be certain of their decision. She wanted their commitment to be for keeps.

The Georgia couple assured Ann and Gary that they were aware of the difficulties ahead—they were prepared for the challenges of raising these two boys into whole and healed men. They were committed. They would care for these boys throughout their childhood.

Two weeks after James and Timmy arrived at their new home—before they had a chance to adjust to their new surroundings—the couple changed their minds. They told Ann, "Gee, we can't do this . . ."

Ann pleaded with them not to disrupt the boys' lives again. She reiterated her willingness to adopt one of the children and begged them to keep one of the boys. Their answer was no. Once again, pleas went out to members of both the McFarland and Smith families to make a commitment to one of the boys. Only Ann and Gary were willing, and in a position to immediately assume the responsibility for a child. Again and again, they begged the Georgia couple to listen to the child welfare specialists and consider alternatives for permanent placement of the boys. Instead, without further word to Ann or Gary, they delivered James and Timmy back to their original foster family.

Ann was devastated. She felt betrayed. She could not conceive of anyone—especially not a family member who claimed commitment and a Christian "calling" to nurture these children—displaying such a disregard for the long-term emotional well-being of her two young nephews.

The machinations of one of the attorneys involved in the custody case left Ann Carr—an attorney in Missouri—with a jaded view of the ethical standards acceptable in Texas legal circles. Even more, she was appalled by the conduct of Sue's divorce lawyer, Christine Tharp, who refused to refund even a portion of the $7,500 deposit Sue paid for her divorce. Any money Tharp returned would have gone to the estate for the care of the boys.

Tharp insisted that she was within her legal rights to keep all of the deposit, because Sue had signed an agreement that stated the deposit was non-refundable. However, Tharp was unable or unwilling to produce a copy of that signed document—or copies of any of the billing documents—when Ann requested them.

To add to Ann's frustration, other Texas lawyers expressed outrage at Tharp's refusal to refund a large portion of the deposit, but were not interested in pursuing the claim on behalf of the boys. More than one of them suggested that Ann should threaten Tharp with a wrongful death action based on the fact that when Tharp gave Sue the disk with the divorce papers, she contributed to Rick's extreme action. Ann's husband Gary wrote letters to the Texas Bar Association about the matter; but, in the end, Ann dropped the battle. It simply was not worth the stress it generated.

His courtroom appearance over in Bexar County, Rick Mc-Farland's transfer to a prison in the Texas Department of Criminal Justice system was the next step in his incarceration. Before he left San Antonio, he called one of Sue's neighborhood friends, Molly Matthews. "I'll be gone for a long time," he said.

Molly, certain the only reason he called was to get information about the boys or to manipulate her into providing updates in the future, snapped a final response: "Look. I do not know anything about your kids. And I am not in touch with them. So don't call me again." She slammed down the phone and tried to shut down her memories to bury her anger, pain and grief.

Indications were that Rick's inability to get along with other inmates continued after he went into the custody of the state. In less than a year, he was housed in three different facilities. He started at the Garza West unit in Beeville—halfway between San Antonio and the Texas Gulf Coast.

Next, he was transferred to the Robertson facility out in Abilene—not "the prettiest town" in Kansas that George Hamilton IV made famous in song, but the one in dusty west Texas out in the middle of nowhere. Then he was moved to the old Ellis unit in Huntsville—the east Texas prison that once housed Death Row.

He was still there at Christmas 2004, where he generated a bounty of holiday letters to neighbors, family, friends and the author of this book. Each one had a short personalized message, but most of the contents were generic. They contained a page torn from an unidentified daily inspirational booklet dated November 14. On some copies, several lines were highlighted, including this one: "The Lord loves us and doesn't want us to gossip about others, even those who have done something wrong." The message from Rick McFarland was as subtle as a tsunami.

Every card contained Rick's handwritten poem, "Christmastide Reflections":

> Sometimes our life is littered with troubles that hold
> us down like a heavyweight—
> Choices we make each day may buildup and direct
> which of life's roads we negotiate.
> With the passage of time, we may come to understand
> that life is not always fair—
> Life is prone to accidental actions, some lead to radi-
> ant rejoice, others to darkest despair.
> 'Tis the Season to maybe stop holding life's negatives,
> let them go, let them escape—
> Christmastide, let's reflect on the life of Jesus Christ,
> whose birth we celebrate!

Many were disgusted that Rick continued to hide behind the Bible. One line in particular, "Life is prone to accidental actions . . ." engendered the most visceral response among the recipients. Some shredded the card and its contents to bits. Others contemplated the appropriateness of another homicide in the McFarland family.

Ann was stressed by the correspondence she received. Her brother Pete was enraged—he did not want Rick bugging his sister anymore.

It was now time to erect a monument on Sue's grave. Ann made one decision that she would not consider changing. The name on the stone would be "Susan Burris Smith." "Rick McFarland defiled that marriage, and I didn't want anything to do with him on that slate," she said.

She did feel, however, that William was old enough to

provide input into the design of the stone. She wanted the memorial to be meaningful to him. William chose carved roses to immortalize his mother's love of that flower. The original suggestion for the inscription used the phrase "beloved mother." William wanted to change that. He wanted the wording to reflect who his mother was instead of how he felt about her. His words were, "Loving mother of William, James and Timothy. Always in our hearts." The stone was installed on December 15.

The boys remain vibrant in the hearts of many. Dreams of their future fill the air with good will—hopes that all three will grow to be happy, productive adults. Linda Schlather, principal of Woodridge Elementary, summed up these feelings well: "I want them to somehow one day forgive their dad enough to gain their own inner peace. I want them to be loved and nurtured. They are bright boys and have great potential—I hope it can be fulfilled."

With the coming of the new year of 2005, Sue's boys, at last, had some of the stability and security that disappeared from their lives the night their mother died. The original foster parents adopted James and Timmy. The two boys had a new family, new names, new lives. All who have seen them report that they are doing well.

William—the child who knew more than he may ever say—longed for goodness and safety. 2005 heralded the first step of this wish. He is in the middle of the adoption process. His new, single, middle-aged mother is devoted to him. With her education and background in child welfare and development, and without the distraction of a husband or other children, she is able to give him the one-on-one attention he needs. She wants him to be able to close the door to the past—but she hopes it is a glass door and he will be able to look back through it and keep his mother alive.

William calls her "Mom." The healing has begun.

Afterword

Throughout the process of researching and writing this book, I was haunted by questions. How could this happen? How could a professional, competent, take-charge woman be manipulated to her death in her own home? How could someone so well-loved by her family, friends, neighbors and co-workers be killed by the person closest to her?

These questions all framed Susan McFarland as a victim—a tragedy in the making—nothing more. Then, after months of hearing stories from those who cared about Susan, a real person took shape in my mind—a complex woman with simple dreams and an unquenchable lust for life.

One morning, while driving up Interstate Highway 35 to Austin, Susan McFarland became so real to me that I thought about how much more I would enjoy the ride if she were sitting beside me sharing stories and passing the time together. Then the realization struck—I would never be able to talk to her. I would never bump into her in Central Market. I would never laugh with her over lunch. I would never hear the sound of her voice or see the sunny glow of her smile.

At that moment, I was struck by a sense of loss so visceral it took my breath away and formed pools of water in my eyes. The light of a life-enriching personality was snuffed out, never to brighten anyone's day again. Gone forever—all because of the violent selfishness of one man.

Beyond her loss of life, the scars inflicted on her three young boys will live forever. Never again will they be able to turn to the unconditional love and support of their mother. Never again can they seek her advice, her approval, her comfort. Surely, Rick McFarland must have understood—and not cared about—what he stole from them on that fatal night.

How can we ever understand him or his motivation? He and Susan created life together—three young lives. How could he plot and plan to take her life away? How can we conceive of a heart that hard—that cold?

Richard McFarland's family was not forthcoming about the events and influences in his childhood that molded him into the man he became. But while in San Antonio, his mother made many remarks that granted a glimpse into a twisted concept of reality that could be the root of it all. Most telling of all was her insistence that Rick had many reasons to justify what he did.

There are those in the community who question why, in the face of Rick's strange personality and bizarre behavior, Susan did not act sooner—that she did not protect her sons better. If she had not hesitated, they insist, she would not have been lost.

But to place blame on Susan is unfair and uninformed. We all sit here with the advantage of a hindsight that Susan did not possess. We all look at the problems in the family from the outside in. From that vantage point, the signs of destruction seem lit with neon. But Sue was in the eye of the storm. In her close-up view, all changes were gradual and slow. All sense of normalcy was skewed in a dysfunctional prism—blurred by the numbing pattern of everyday life.

Yes, to some extent, she was in denial—blinded by an intense desire to have a normal marriage and family—crippled by her determination to take charge and fix all that was wrong. Most of us have, at one point or another, used denial as a coping mechanism for dealing with circumstances beyond our control. Many of us have stuck with a stubborn persistence in a belief that we could rectify a situation that is beyond repair.

Susan had passed through that place and entered another. She had a plan in mind. She was moving forward.

There is no way to be sure that any different or quicker action by Sue would have changed the outcome. No matter when she'd made the decision to leave—whether at the time she did, or two years earlier—Rick might still have set his plan into motion and acted upon it without warning. He was a passive-aggressive manipulator, who orchestrated the scenario that unfolded at 351 Arcadia. Once he realized she was going to leave, and he decided that was not acceptable, there was no line he would not cross.

Sue was a planner, arranging with infinite detail for every eventuality before she made her move. She wanted to create the least disruption and trauma for her boys as possible. She even found housing for the husband she intended to evict from her home. If she had been more impulsive and just fled with her boys in the middle of the night, would she still be alive? Maybe. Maybe not.

The fact is that the most dangerous time for any woman is that transition period from when she decides to leave, through the months of the separation. That is when many women are battered. That is when many women die. Statistics show that separated women are three times more likely than divorced women, and twenty-five times more likely than married women still living with their husbands, to be victimized.

In 2002, the year of Susan's death, 117 women in Texas were killed by a husband or a boyfriend. While women are less likely than men to be victims of violent crime overall, they are five to eight times more likely to be victimized by their intimate partner. On average, more than three women are murdered by those men in this country every day.

Even if Sue had managed to keep her divorce a secret from her husband until the papers were served, she had no statistical guarantee that her fate would have changed, because of the elevated risk to her safety during the estrangement period. It is just as likely that a man in Richard McFarland's state of mind may have made the same murder plans after he was forced from the family home as he did while he still resided there.

Susan McFarland did not imagine her divorce would be

free of conflict, but she did not envision the fatal consequences that did result. It is my fervent wish that her story not be repeated again.

It is my hope that you have learned from reading this book and are now more aware of the warning signs of destruction and more cognizant of the risk of violence.

I hope, if the need arises, you will be able to use this knowledge to save your life or to save the life of someone dear to you.

That is my prayer.